YOUR LIFE IN THE METAVERSE

GIDEON BURROWS

REALLY INTERESTING BOOKS

Please report any errors to gideon@ngomedia.org.uk

To Simon Whittacker, for offering technical advice and always supporting my work

CONTENTS

INTRODUCTION

Imagine a world where almost everything you do is online. After breakfast, you pull on a headset and sensory gloves. You check your feed - it contains all your emails, WhatsApp messages, posts, texts, and recorded messages. Only, there's no difference between them. It's just 'communicating'. Most times, the person who's left you a message appears as a video.

Only that video message is from a computerized version of their face. Their 'avatar'. You can see in all the messages and the video, a high definition floating hologram. The messages are from friends and family, some local marketing, some spam messages.

You use your hands to swipe away the trash using your sensory gloves, then settle in for three or four minutes of reading, hearing and viewing messages.

You then record a few messages yourself. Your own avatar will show up when your friends next check in. That's likely to be right away or in the next few minutes. You send a few email messages yourself, speaking the text, instead of typing. It all appears before you, perfectly spelled. The system recognizes your voice and knows your intonations well enough. It can get a next to perfect version of what you want to say.

The system might even improve what you want to say: adding more emphasis, powerful words and phrases, depending on whether you're messaging your mom, your boss or your child's teacher. It will have learned who these people are and will adjust accordingly.

Now it's time to work. There's a 9 a.m. meeting, and you swipe your hand to enter the virtual chat room. Before you, you see six workmates gathered around the table. Only, you're seeing their avatars. Computer generated versions of your colleagues in their work-mode - clothing and presentation appropriate for your online workspace. Probably not the comedy avatar you use when you meet with your children and friends. You greet your fellow avatars, and go through the latest sales results, or plans for the local council, or the patients you are treating, or the community event you are putting together.

In the center of the table, you can all see a clear image floating. It's a financial graph, perhaps. A proposal for a brand identity. Some designs for a poster. A copy of the local legislation you need to edit.

You discuss it with fellow avatars, and the image is manipulated and edited in real time. Until you and your colleagues are satisfied. You swipe the graphic to your boss, or civil servant, or marketing team. Each of your team prints off a copy of the logo, or poster, or legislation in the real world on their printers at home, or store it on their virtual wall in their home office. If you are designing an object, perhaps you'll print a 3D version in the real world. The meeting is over. You sign off.

The online meeting has saved you time, so you take a

moment to browse an online toyshop for your daughter's birthday. From your 'home life' screen, you select ToysToGo, and virtually enter the shop. Directly before you are toys appropriate to her age. The shop already has a profile of you. It shows you 3D projections of the toys most suitable for your family. No plastics, no fake guns. Yes to dinosaurs, prince and princesses, puzzles and the latest online games.

The virtual shop has already screened out things you've bought before. It won't show you things it knows you don't want to buy or don't have a track record of looking at previously. Though it offers you a search bar, as well as a 'speak to search' function, in case you want to explore deeper into the shop.

You call for 'soccer'. An entire shelf of soccer related toys hurtles towards you in 3D. You swipe a kid's soccer shirt. It appears already in your daughter's size. A matching pair of shorts appear, though you didn't request them. Both go into a virtual shopping basket. An avatar (of a race and gender an algorithm has decided is most likely to ensure you complete the transaction) smiles as money is taken from your account in Metacoin. They thank you for your business today. You swipe one of five hovering buttons to say how satisfied you are with your shop.

Ten minutes have gone by, and you swipe back into your office. There's a report to write, and numerous feeds to respond to. Virtual meetings to prepare for. It's going to be a busy day, so you decide to pre-order your lunch. You pull up your company's menu and a cabinet of 3D versions of the dishes on offer appear. You select what you want by swiping them onto a virtual tray and set the time you want it to be delivered in the real world by bicycle courier.

During the day, the system you're using reminds you to take screen breaks. It lets you know when your heartbeat is too high or your blood pressure is too low, or your sugar levels are awry. It already knows you're short on your medication. A feed appears in the afternoon from the avatar of your online pharmacist asking you to approve re-issue of the drugs.

Your drugs will be delivered with your next weekly shop delivery. You will be reminded tonight about your shopping before the final list is created. All your usual grocery items will appear on a virtual shelf before you. If you turn your head, you will see other items. Things you have bought before. You can swipe items onto your shopping list, or off them, and they will move across visually, the cost in Metacoin changing in real time.

You can choose new items, using the voice or text search box you're familiar with from the toy shop. You exit the virtual shop and your Metacoin is charged automatically. The goods will be delivered by a zero-emissions electric vehicle. It's five years since you had your own car.

After lunch, you virtually visit the gym for a half an hour session of cardio work. Among other avatars you've come to know - all at the same level as you - you do crouches, press ups, leg stretches, jumping jacks. Your coach, which is the avatar of a real life coach in his own studio, sees your avatar's movements and he is able to offer advice.

Work is over by mid-afternoon. Time to see the kids. They've been in the room next door. In their own virtual classrooms, in their own virtual schools. Their teachers have been delivering real time lessons, and your children have been typing in the air, swiping, putting up their hands, and speaking out loud to their teachers. Inside their headsets, their own school avatars have been in class with those of their fellow pupils. Your son says the best lesson today was music, where he played virtual guitar.

You have an offline family meal together, and your older child asks if he can meet online with his friends afterwards. He goes into his room, pulls on his headset, selects his social avatar, and is gone for an hour. Your daughter pulls on her own headset and visits the virtual library, swiping between books - appropriate for her age, her reading level, and according to the rules you have virtually discussed with the online librarian (an automated bot, this time, rather than a real person). No romance; no guns; mild bad language permitted. Fact and fiction allowed, especially soccer and books on a reading list set by her schoolteacher.

Your daughter downloads the book she wants and sits on her bed as she virtually flips through the pages, her hands swinging in the air. While she reads, other anonymized readers of the same book are leaving voice, avatar, and text messages, discussing the book in real time. Your daughter responds to a few. The whole chat is monitored remotely by the system, to ensure language is measured and fair, and any spam is immediately deleted.

While the kids are engaged, you check the shopping list, then scroll through the film network to find something you'd like to watch tonight. Once they're in bed, you join a friend who you've messaged about the film. Your avatars meet in the virtual cinema. Your share a face-to-face chat using your avatars. The hand movements you make are mirrored in the virtual world. The film begins, and you settle in with a dozen other avatars to watch first the advertising, then the movie. You could have selected to watch any film, and there would likely be others around the world who wanted to watch that same film too. You could have chosen to watch the film in any virtual setting: your sofa with your friend, a large screen movie theater full of other avatars, an outside big screen, even a hotel room. But you always remembered how much you enjoyed the cinema.

This is the metaverse.

Or at least, this is one version of the metaverse. No-one knows how the metaverse will look. But it will certainly involve a headset, lots of virtual reality 3D experiences, online payments and currencies, and social media that is far more immersive than we have.

In my short scenario, I have attempted to illustrate in a general way how the metaverse might look. But I've also taken the opportunity to raise what some of the challenges and pitfalls might be. You may gain from less work time, and being able to share work virtually with colleagues without having to travel. But your time with your kids, in real life, might be sacrificed. You may squeeze in some virtual exercise. But is that as good as going outside for a jog?

Sure, shopping virtually is convenient, quick and probably cheaper than it is in the real world. But will you get the choice you'd like? Do you think it's okay that the supermarket knows what you want before you do? Or that it makes judgements about your appetites and preferences, based on huge amounts of data you've provided to the metaverse simply by being part of it?

It's great to quickly get your prescriptions virtually, but who sees that data? Your pharmacist is a robot, not an individual. How does that feel? Do you trust the system to make the right decisions for you?

And you sure enjoyed that film with your buddy. But would you have enjoyed it more if you had seen her? Shared her warmth, seen and felt the emotion of the movie together. Picked up her own signals of happiness, or even distress in her failing relationship, which you couldn't possibly pick up virtually. Or perhaps you can?

That's the challenge of the metaverse. The scenario I've sketched out aims to give us a taste of how the metaverse might be. But it may well not look like this. It is 'emergent'. Like the slow growth of the internet and social media, by degrees it will come, we will get used to it, and rely on it. And then we will look forward to what else it can do for us. There will not be a day when the metaverse is 'switched on'.

This book aims to outline what the metaverse might look like as it develops in the next five to ten years. It is likely to affect every one of us in the higher income world, whether we like it or not. It will bring huge benefits and convenience, it's likely to help cut CO_2 emissions and increase productivity at work, in education, and in our own lives. But it is not without its challenges.

I hope here to give you an idea of what to expect. I hope to prompt questions in your own mind about how deeply you will allow the metaverse to affect your life. How can you take advantage? How can you benefit from the development of the technology and the opportunities? What loss of rights, privacy and comfort will you need to accept in order to immerse yourself?

Welcome to the metaverse.

Who is this book for?

This is a basic introductory book about the metaverse. In October 2021, I ran a straw poll among Facebook friends. This is what I posted:

"Very quick answer please. Don't think about it. Don't be embarrassed. Don't look it up. Don't look at others' comments. It's for my research. I'd be most grateful. Ready? What is The Metaverse?"

The answers were as diverse as they were funny.

- *No idea!*
- *Meta-, all-encompassing, -verse, like in universe, so all places together.*
- *Heard of it but still no clue!!*
- *Parallel universe?*
- *It's the interconnected universe between media properties, mostly fuelled via crossover events, right?*
- *A poetic metaphor?*
- *It's a Neal Stephenson thing: cyberspace.*
- *Do you report directly to Mr Z?*
- *I'm guessing it's the space outside the universe, like Philip Pullman's Dark Materials where there's parallel universes or maybe Pratchett's Discworld where the universe is just an object like a marble in a room full of other universes. Or not?*
- *It's the world you plug into with your online avatar. Like in Ready Player One.*
- *It is being used to describe an alternative universe that exists online. Typically, a 3D sandbox style gaming environment. Second Life was an early example of a metaverse.*

Then it just got silly, with some naughty responses I needn't share here. Only a few of my Facebook friends at that time 'got' the metaverse as I understood it. Some didn't know what I was writing about.

Others mistook it for the ethereal '*multi*verse' which is the idea that our universe is only one of an infinite number of universes, somehow stacked alongside, or within, or on top of each other. Our universe could be one of millions underneath an alien's fingernail. That kind of mind blowing stuff. (Those as old as me might remember this idea from the end of Will Smith's fantastic action movie, Men In Black.)[1]

Yet, the metaverse, when you try to pin it down, *can* feel just as imprecise. No-one knows exactly what it is, how it will develop, what it will look like when we have it, and whether we'll know when its arrived. Even the last two responses (I grouped them together) are close, but don't quite agree with each other.

No wonder people are confused.

I'd been considering writing a book on the metaverse for a few months, and finally decided that I would by asking my friends if they even knew what it was.

Then days later the co-founder and CEO of Facebook, Mark Zuckerberg, announced on October 28, 2021, that his company would be changing its name to 'Meta'. He would be taking his Meta - and the brands the company owns - Facebook, Instagram, WhatsApp, Oculus (the virtual reality headset company) and more - further into the interconnected online space he called the metaverse.

His announcement by letter to his colleagues, along with a rather stilted one hour 20 minutes keynote video released to the world, indicated the direction he envisioned the company would move. It remained quite technical, and much of the internet discussion about the metaverse has been technical too.

As I write, no-one is quite sure what the metaverse will look like. Not even Mark Zuckerberg. No-one knows which internet, and other companies will be involved, how internet users will react, and how online creators will be able to use it.

That's fine. When we started getting cell phones, no-one

could have envisaged that actually *talking* to people using them would become as rare as it is now.

When English computer scientist Tim Berners-Lee proposed the idea in 1980 of creating hypertext, a kind of clickable and shareable text between computers so researchers could share and update data, he didn't envisage his ideas would develop into the World Wide Web, and then the so called internet. Let alone that his system would emerge into a full on shopping, entertainment, commerce, information, learning and sharing platform.

In 2003, when Mark Zuckerberg and a bunch of other computer keen students at Harvard set up a website so others could judge the looks of fellow students, their plans were no more than that. No-one was aiming for, or even imagined, Facebook would become what it is today.

Nor that Facebook would become a prime mover in what pundits are calling Web 3.0 - the metaverse.

Ironically, the platforms mentioned above have given us the opportunity to discuss and even influence the future of online and offline communications before they actually happen. Or at least *as* they happen. Those opportunities were a lot tougher before widespread mobile communications, the internet, social media, and Facebook.

There are already technical books about each element of what is likely to become the metaverse. There are also many other books, videos, discussions and arguments to come. There are books aimed at coders and technical enthusiasts. At politicians and academics. At philosophers and futurists.

This is not one of those books.

This is a non-technical book about the metaverse for those of us who use social media and gaming tools like Facebook, Minecraft, and Pinterest, but don't know the detail of how they're run, nor do we care that much.

I have written about social media, including two novels in which the future of social media and its implications comes into question.

Your Life In The Metaverse aims to give us all a basic, but clear, understanding of your own role and lives in the metaverse. Most of us will gradually see the emergence of the metaverse in our lifetime, probably in the next ten to 15 years.

You're probably not particularly interested in coding. You don't know what an API or a blockchain is (yet!) It doesn't matter. This book is for you.

The book is not aimed at big-brained computer programers or politicians or even company CEOs. Though I also hope these may benefit from examining the metaverse in its most basic terms. The metaverse is happening, and all of us in the modernized world will be affected one way or another, even those who attempt to go 'off grid'.

I hope from these pages, you'll take away solid information about how the metaverse will change and influence your daily life: from how you work to how your kids are educated; from where and how you get your information, to how you book vacations and travel; from how you spend your leisure time (and leisure money) to how your own home may be designed to accommodate the metaverse; from how you keep in touch with your family and friends, to how you share yourself, your news, your life with the outside world. And a whole lot more besides.

Alongside, I aim to outline what some of the ethical and privacy concerns about the metaverse might be. If you're already concerned about the amount of data that private companies have about you and your family, or how you always seem to be targeted with advertising that seems to fit the things you're particularly interested in, then you might want to see how these things are likely to develop in the metaverse. Perhaps you are concerned about freedom of speech, security of your finances, bullying and extremist opinions.

If you are not reading for that reason, you may come to understand why you might consider them. It will be for you - not me - to decide how worried or relaxed you should be.

All I assume is that you probably do have internet access, that you have a mobile phone that you generally use more than to talk to your family. You've bought shopping online. You may have booked travel. You may well have gamed, or even attended a video call or conference. You're likely to understand that companies like Apple, Facebook (now called Meta), Google and Amazon, and the platforms you use, are big players.

If you have done any or all of these things, it is likely you already have the experience you need to understand what the metaverse is. Anything else, I will explain.

If I miss anything out, or assume too much knowledge, please do email or message me - there I am, already assuming you know what even *those* things are - and I'll add in clarity in future issues.

Defining the metaverse?

The metaverse is not something written down on a document that companies and individuals are working towards. It isn't a goal, set in digital stone, that everyone is working on achieving, and once they achieve it, we will all be able to say: 'Welcome metaverse, what took you so long?'

The metaverse is an ongoing, morphing development of

the internet, as well as the way individuals, communities, governments, and corporations interact.

Or to put in more simply, and this is my own rather clumsy attempt:

> *"The metaverse is what the internet will look like, and feel like, during the next ten to 15 years, though it is already developing rapidly. It is likely to be a 3D virtual experience you can interact with using a virtual reality and augmented reality headset and sensory gloves, perhaps with cameras and sensors tracking your body movements. It will allow you to carry out the functions for which you currently use all parts of the internet and mobile communications. But also, much more besides. Most importantly, the metaverse will be its own internal world which will continue whether you are logged on or not, and it will also be fully integrated into our everyday lives. It will be engaged with the world outside the metaverse, and the world outside the metaverse will be engaged by it."*

Many believe the metaverse will have virtual reality (VR) at its center. That's when we pull on glasses or goggles and 'walk around' in a 3D version of the world, accessing tools, playing games, going about our business. Many may have experienced this at theme parks, or at the bowling alley. Some at home, with computer games. Only a few of us might have joined a virtual reality meeting using a headset.

But virtual reality is one way of looking at the metaverse. VR is likely to play a huge part in the future internet, but it is going to be so much more than simply making a 3D version of what most of us already do in 2D when we scroll up and down computer screens, or punch buttons on our cell phones.

The metaverse is about communications and interaction

in all of our lives. And all of those opportunities being in a single place, and easily accessible. Some of that will be a virtual experience, but a lot more will be about how we interact within the metaverse, and with others using the opportunities it offers.

Let's have a look at what some experts and commentators have said the metaverse is. They don't all agree.

Ironically, we turn to Wikipedia first, perhaps in itself an embodiment of the ideas behind the metaverse. It is a gathered space for information that anyone can contribute to, edit, monitor, gain from, and share. Note, by the nature of Wikipedia, the definition I write here may well have changed by the time you read this book.

> *"The metaverse is the hypothesized next iteration of the internet, supporting decentralized, persistent online 3D virtual environments. This virtual space will be accessible through virtual reality headsets, augmented reality glasses, smartphones, PCs, and game consoles. The metaverse has well defined use cases within the video game, business, education, retail, and real estate sectors."*[2]

Matthew Ball is a venture capitalist, former Head of Strategy for Amazon Studios, and an expert and commentator on the emergence of the metaverse. He writes:

> *"The metaverse is the next generation of the internet: it enables creators to deliver connected, immersive experiences based around activities... Many people think of the metaverse as 3D space that will surround us. But the metaverse is not 3D or 2D or even necessarily graphical; it is about the inexorable dematerialization of physical space, distance, and objects... We*

will transpose a life of looking at computers from the outside, to one of being inside the virtual world and it being all around us."[3]

Jon Radoff, a metaverse commentator and experienced writer on gaming, defines the metaverse as follows:

"The next generation of the internet. It's a next generation that's already in progress, we're already living in it. It's something we have right now. Some of the defining characteristics is it's decentralized, it's about activities and experiences, more so than transactions, and it's really driven by an enormous number of creators that are making content and making experiences for the metaverse... It's about having experiences, having activities to do, it's about being a person in a space, being yourself there, and that's a little bit different than most of the internet so far."

Mark Zuckerberg, CEO Meta (formerly Facebook), said in an interview with TheVerge:[4]

"I think this is a persistent, synchronous environment where we can be together, which I think is probably going to resemble some kind of hybrid between the social platforms that we see today, but an environment where you're embodied in it."

And then there is the mainstream media:

"The digital and the physical are inextricably intertwined in an all-encompassing virtual reality that allows all of us to exist together, whenever and wherever."

Molly Roberts, Washington Post [5]

> *"Instead of being on a computer, in the metaverse you might use a headset to enter a virtual world connecting all sorts of digital environments. Unlike current virtual reality, which is mostly used for gaming, this virtual world could be used for practically anything - work, play, concerts, cinema trips - or just hanging out. Most people envision that you would have a 3D avatar - a representation of yourself - as you use it. But because it's still just an idea, there's no single agreed definition of the metaverse."*
>
> *BBC News Website*[6]

Matthew Ball's book, *The Metaverse: And How it Will Revolutionize Everything*, due out in Summer 2022, is likely to be the go-to text for professionals interested in the future of the internet. In a seminal series of essays on the metaverse, *The Metaverse Primer,* he identifies what its core attributes are likely to be:[7]

Persistent - it will continue to exist, it won't reset, pause, or end. It will just be there;

Synchronous and live - though there will be set time events like concerts, work meetings and video gatherings, the metaverse will continue as a lived ongoing experience that can be accessed any time;

Each user will have an individual sense of presence - everyone can join in and have their own experience, which will be theirs alone, though they may interact with others during those experiences;

A fully functioning economy - virtual money will be exchanged, traded, assets will be bought and sold, and virtual 'work' will be carried out in the metaverse in exchange for 'value' that is recognized by others;

Will span the real and digital world - the metaverse is not an online experience only. It will interact with the real world, influencing and being influenced by what is happening offline;

Offer unprecedented interoperability - companies, designers, individuals, and users will work together, and interact together, to build and experience the universe. The silo mentality of individual companies and brands will be broken down. A 'skin' bought on Fortnite might be traded on Facebook, or worn by a player in a FIFA game;

Created and operated by a wide range of contributors - not only the big internet companies, but new emerging companies specializing in the virtual and online space, as well as individuals and entrepreneurs, who will use tools established within the metaverse to grow it, provide new opportunities, and to gain from it.

What is the metaverse in a technical sense?

An easy way to understand what the metaverse might be, is to picture how we have previously interacted with internet companies.

Say you have a Facebook account. Every time you 'check Facebook', your interactions are with the one company. Your data and interaction happens through Facebook, and other individual's interactions also happen through Facebook too. The platform might make you *feel* and even believe you're interacting directly with your friends, customers, and followers, but your relationship is via the middle operator: Facebook.

Another example. You (or more likely your kids or young adults) have a Fortnite account, the gaming platform. You log on to play the game, communicate with others, hang out, and buy stuff with V-bucks (which is Fortnite's currency). But your interactions are still via the Fortnite platform. Your connection is direct between Fortnite and your PlayStation or X-Box, not directly with your friend or another player's computer.

Another example. You shop at Target. You use the Target website to select the goods you want. You pay Target through their payment system, which Target has commissioned to take payments on its behalf. Target then sends your goods out to you. Your relationship is directly between Target and you, via your computer or mobile device.

Internet companies have spent the last ten years talking about 'the cloud', when in fact they have meant *their* cloud. My data on Facebook is stored on Facebook's cloud. My Mac backs up the words I'm typing onto Apple's cloud. Amazon stores my book buying and selling data on Amazon's cloud. (Though, in truth Amazon's services provide the majority of online space for other companies.)

The metaverse posits something different.

Instead of single nodules or silos (company, game, shop), with each computer having a direct relationship with its customers, the metaverse is likely to be a huge network of interaction, with untold numbers of connections between many, many participants. Instead of many clouds, the metaverse might end up being the one single cloud we've been led to imagine.

This is not the World Wide Web. To compare it to a spider's web is even too narrow, because the connections in a web are too neat, the strands all meeting in regular patterns and moving towards a middle.

The metaverse will be more like an enormous ball of wool dropped on the floor, with billions of channels of interaction that won't rely on communicating directly with a single company or strand. It will just be general communication and interaction.

Metaverse commentator Jon Radoff has created a (2D) mind map of what he envisages the metaverse will include, and how different aspects will link and sprout from each other. It illustrates the many dozens of avenues the future of the internet will encompass, from every day easier-to-understand ideas like multiplayer games and immersive shopping, to tech speak most users of the metaverse will not even need to understand, such as self-sovereign identity, decentralized applications, and exchanges, and modding.[8]

Companies, big and small, right down to single individuals, will communicate with each other, build on each other's work, and the metaverse will be an ever growing and developing space. This space will be 'hosted' on the internet, literally in electronic servers in huge warehouses, probably enormous expansions of the servers and storage used by all the big internet companies.

Or at least that's one theory.

It is yet to be clear how far the various big companies such as Facebook, Epic Games and Amazon will want to 'hold on' to their direct channels, and their clouds? Will they continue creating small nodules within the bunch of wool, forcing users to go through them, instead of letting it all go free? More on this later.

Let's start at the beginning.

EXPLORING THE METAVERSE

It's a Neal Stephenson thing: cyberspace, right?

The correspondent responding to my Facebook straw poll had it right on the money when he mentioned sci-fi author Neal Stephenson. His 1992 novel *Snow Crash*, said to be the first reference to a 'metaverse', envisaged the next generation of the internet. The snow crash of the title represents the fuzzy snowy screen a Mac computer used to display when the program you were using crashed.

In the novel, the world has gone dystopian, governments and economies have crashed, and the only means of escape is into a computer-generated universe of virtual reality known as the metaverse, via a virtual reality headset and headphones.

Participants create avatars in order to communicate with each other in the metaverse. But a computer bug, also named Snow Crash, is now making that platform untenable, threatening the future of human interaction. Stephenson's metaverse features an online encrypted currency and explores the idea of using that money to buy online real estate.

The author told online tech magazine Axios he has never had any contact with Mark Zuckerberg or Facebook about his book, though he has seen his concept developing over the last thirty years by other companies.

"Good science fiction tries to depict futures that are plausible enough to seem persuading to the readers - many of whom are technically savvy, and tough critics. So, when depicting a future technology in a work of science fiction, you have to make it plausible. And if it's plausible enough, it can be implemented in the real world."[1]

You will be able to read more about Stephenson's world later in this book, along with information about metaverse type ideas in other books and movies.

A history of the metaverse

Aside from popular culture, which shouldn't be discounted as an influence on our imagination about what the future might look like - Marty McFly's hoverboard anyone? - the history of the metaverse has been one of continual technological development, rather than once in a lifetime world-changing inventions.

Some commentators argue we are already in the first stages of the metaverse, and our transition to it will be seamless development, rather than landing at a particular spot. When we arrive there, we might not know it, and might already be on our way to whatever proceeds it.

But let's look backwards, before looking ahead.

Wikipedia offers a list of major milestones on the way to the development of the metaverse. Up until more recent years, the main players in these stages didn't know their work would be contributing to what the metaverse is likely to become. Some of the developments listed by Wikipedia are about technical coding language, so I've taken them out as too complex to cover here.

Suffice to say, they are the 'inside the box' coding of shareable information and coding standards, which allow one computer to talk to another in 'the same language' about how to create things and respond to things in 3D. That goes back at least as far as 1978. Imagine it as bicycle manufacturers coming to an agreement, as they did, that a single link in a basic bike chain is exactly one inch long, and standard wheel sizes come in 24, 26 and 28 inches. Though, just like in the technology world - Microsoft vs Apple? - there's remains lots of incompatibility in the bicycle industry too.

- 1993 – Steve Jackson Games created a text-based virtual reality system, in which users could discuss everything related to science fiction, fantasy, comics, and gaming. They could also upload their own coding, for editing and critique.
- 1995 – Active Worlds was launched, based entirely on Snow Crash. It enabled users to visit virtual reality worlds, exploring environments and buildings that others had created, and enabling users to build their own.
- 2003 – Second Life was launched by Linden Lab, to create a 3D online space in which people can interact, play, do business, and otherwise communicate.
- 2006 – Roblox was published, a gaming platform

in which users can play games, and also create their own which can be shared with other users.

- 2017 - Epic games launches Fortnite, a gaming system based on 3D interaction. It is only about playing games.
- 2018 – A multi-player online multiverse game called NeosVR was launched by Solirax.
- 2019 – Facebook Horizon was announced as a social virtual world by Facebook. At time of writing, it is still in the beta (testing) phase, and runs on Microsoft as well as in Facebook's own virtual reality system, called Oculus.
- 2020 – Decentraland was launched as a decentralized virtual platform owned and operated by its users.
- 2021 – Epic Games directs funding to build out Fortnite into a metaverse.
- 2021 – Microsoft Mesh, a mixed reality software enabling virtual presence through Microsoft devices such as the HoloLens 2, was announced.
- 2021 – South Korea announces the creation of a national metaverse alliance with the goal to build a unified national virtual and augmented reality platform.
- 2021 – The parent company of the social network Facebook is renamed from "Facebook, Inc". to "Meta Platforms", indicating the most significant internet platform was pushing into the future with extra gusto.

Gaming and popular media have had a huge influence on the development of interactive and 3D internet, and you can find out more about the contribution of Roblox,

SecondLife, Fortnite and others later on in the book, as well as the vision of books, films, and art.

What is clear is that the metaverse will rely and be built on our increasing comfort and trust with interacting with virtual worlds, or 'virtual mainstreaming'.

As Jon Radoff writes: "As trust continues to increase in the 'virtual' realm — with online friends, virtual items and crypto assets, smart contracts, and live online experiences — it will increase the scalability of the metaverse and the industries that support it."[2]

Please note: Throughout this book I will be writing about Meta and Facebook. Since October 2021, the company previously called Facebook. Inc. changed its name to Meta Platforms. However, the platform Meta owns, called Facebook, remains as it is. When I write about Meta, I mean the parent company. When I write about Facebook I either mean the platform that remains Facebook, or Facebook before it's rename. In most cases, it won't matter.

Looking back, looking forward

You should now be getting the impression that the metaverse, though popular as an idea just now, is really nothing new. It has been an ongoing, interactive process, and will continue to be. Think of it as an ongoing game of Lego, in which new pieces are gradually introduced and older pieces fall out of fashion.

Developers have been playing with this *technical* Lego for many years, building, adapting, joining up their structures, breaking others, re-adapting, re-building, adding new emergent parts, and taking away things that no longer work. The metaverse won't be a new set of Lego, apart from what we already have. It will be the further addition of new parts, continually rebuilt and adapted over time.

I am, at time of writing, 44 years old. That makes me Generation X, son of the baby boom generation, and just about parent of Generation Y or those babies who saw in the Millennium.

That means I grew up in times when you actually had to pick up a phone attached to a wall, to make a call to a number you had to remember or write down. My family shared an Amstrad PCW computer, which was a glorified typewriter, which saved the little pre-teen magazine I wrote on flexible floppy disks of 5 inches square. We had an Atari gaming computer with Daley Thomson's decathlon on it, and my brother and I had worn out the keys by making a tiny digital pixelated Thomson run and then jump.

There was no internet. Computers didn't plug into our house phone line. My dad had a chunky car phone, that had to be plugged into the car, and it had a long aerial. He was an early adopter, which meant he had no-one to call but us at home.

When I reached university, the internet was emerging. We had one central computer in our college library that was white text on a black screen, and it could only be used to search for books. It did, however, connect somehow with the rest of the university's library system, so Tim Berners-Lee must have already worked some of his internet magic by then.

In fact, I had a huge desktop computer in my own university digs by the time my second year rolled round. I could dial in to the internet - buzz, brrr, buzz - to check email (a series of numbers, followed by an @ symbol, then my college name), and to find a limited amount of information on AltaVista or Ask Jeeves. I remember the first item I ever bought online, a book about Pop Art. I still have it. I still haven't read it.

My eldest child is currently thirteen. Ever since their birth we have been able to order shopping, find out times to visit the zoo, book train journeys and email friends and family, at the click of a mouse (remember them?) on a relatively high speed internet connection.

He got his first mobile phone when he was 11, and like with his laptop, has comfortably used it to communicate with friends, search for information, post pictures and homework, listen to music, watch films, and design his own image in 3D form online.

My other son, now 11, has a full virtual presence on Fortnite, including his own 'skin', tools, and buildings, via PlayStation. He also has his own football team on FIFA 21, and he and his elder sibling build worlds together on Minecraft.

My youngest is five. She has her own online school presence, complete with a picture of her online avatar. During Covid, she learned via online lessons, where she could interact with her teacher and classmates. She uses an online platform to 'dress' virtual dolls and characters. Her ability to find stuff on Netflix is far quicker than mine.

And we're not even *that* plugged in as a family.

None of my children have any idea what a dial up internet connection sounds like. Apart from at the excellent Museum of Computing, in Cambridge UK, none have ever seen an Atari, a Gameboy, or a desk top computer. Nor have they ever used a CD to play a game or load a computer program.

All this talk is nothing new, though it might bring a smile to our faces.

The truth is, none of us know what the future of the internet might look like. We're talking about the metaverse, but its final form will be different to what we envisage.

Back then when I was typing out stories on my Amstrad, I had no idea that I might one day be able to type on the tiny (out of date) MacBook Air I have now in front of me. And that as I write, I could double check spelling, facts, and look up new information in real time on Google, rather than waiting for the weekend and hoping one of the books in my local library would somehow contain what I wanted.

The future of technology was unknown, and some great ideas - Segway anyone? - fell by the wayside. Just as other previously unthought of ideas like Wikipedia, Facebook or Google Maps might become near overnight successes that we refer to every day.

Second, some ideas from way-back-when, have stood the test of time, or have come back in different ways, and are likely to be represented once again in the emerging metaverse. In this sense, the metaverse reaches far before Stephenson's Snow Crash, or my pre-dial up internet life.

Take radio. Many feared the radio would be killed off, with the emergence and dominance of new technology like computers and higher definition color TV.

Freddie Mercury and his band Queen lamented its possible death in Radio Gaga: "Let's hope you never leave, old friend/Like all good things, on you we depend/So stick around, 'cause we might miss you/When we grow tired of all this visual/... Radio, what's new? Radio, someone still loves you."

Or as The Buggles put it in 1979: "Video killed the radio star/In my mind and in my car/We can't rewind, we've gone too far/Pictures came and broke your heart/Put the blame on VCR."

But radio did not go away. In fact, it increased, and importantly it merged with new technology. We can use our computers and mobile devices to interact with most radio stations in the world, in whatever language we wish to listen, as they broadcast not only over the airwaves, but also over the internet.

Many of the books we all read and appreciated are now consumed more conveniently as eBooks while we jog, sit on a train, or drive to work.

Note too, the huge increase in recent years, of the podcast, probably the most unlikely of mediums we might expect in an era of bright lights and visuals. We want our information through our ears, we want to hear - not just see - debate, new ideas, investigations, commentary, and story. Whatever the metaverse develops into, it is likely that it will need to reflect the enduring history of our needing to hear, not just see.

Video (and the internet) did not kill the radio star. It gave it, and will continue to give it, new ways to be heard.

Another phenomenon from the past, which has survived the test of time, and which is likely to form a huge part of the metaverse to come, is the encyclopedia. The storage, recording, transition, sharing and absorption of information and data. If anything, that was what computers in their earliest states did: computed information, stored it, and allowed us to read it.

Tim Berners-Lee and the other architects of the internet wanted to share and store research and information more conveniently, over longer distances, and the platform we now know as the World Wide Web came into being.

The information we used to get from 24 leather-bound

heavy thick books in our lounge, quickly moved online where it could be constantly updated and added to, and could be accessed more democratically.

I'd like to say Wikipedia (and the subject specific other '-paedias') is the pinnacle of this, where individuals can add to the world's biggest encyclopaedia, create their own pages, add and edit pages, and share them, but the golden rule I hope we're all beginning to understand now is who knows what weird and wonderful things are to come.

Easy access to masses of information is bound to be an important central aspect of the metaverse. The question of whether that information is always true, unbiased, and correct is something discussed later in this book.

And one final aspect - there are so many others I could have chosen - from our technology past that has endured, and may continue into the future, is the storage - and perhaps immutability - of data.

If you are of my generation, or even before, you may remember recording mix tapes from the radio: Record/Play at the start of the track you wanted, then pressing a clunky Pause button at the end, to catch the end of the music. Then onto another track we liked and wanted to record. We were able to store that data for re-use, and for sharing.

Likewise, we created simple documents, coding, sets of data, that was stored in magnetic form on floppy discs, then gradually in digital form on USB storage devices, and now in the digital 'cloud' to which we upload our information. These days it's hard to delete data. In the past, we could sometimes hear a scratchy version of the tracks on the cassette we were recording over. These days, most data we try to delete still exists somewhere, in the depths of our computers, on our own personal server spaces, or in the wider cloud.

These days, we don't even have to put our credit card details into PayPal or Google Pay. Our systems have remembered that data, and we sign off payments with a click or a simple password. Also stored as remote data.

Into the future, the metaverse will be all about data. Not only the data that circulates around interconnected Apps and programs and virtual worlds, but the data we upload for storage and use. More importantly, as we work more and more in the virtual space, we will be creating new data - our avatars, our currency, our work files, our holidays - within the metaverse that never actually leaves it. Virtual data in a virtual world, completely separate from our real life existence.

That's the kind of data that will endure. It will never go away, because theoretically at least - and perhaps this will be an important decision to be made about the metaverse - we might be able to 'scroll' back the version of the metaverse we access by one day, or two days, or two months. The data we used to have, or we have attempted to delete, will suddenly come back.

The metaverse is the continuing iteration of many uses of technology we've had or desired in the past. Some of our uses and desires have lost their legs, while others have been realized. Meantime, the developing internet and the metaverse has and will continue to create functions we never actually knew we wanted.

Such as the opportunity to create our own videos in our home that could be broadcast to the world in less than 60 seconds, or even live. Or our work and even physical position being tracked by our bosses every minute during working hours (and out of them). Or to play complex games of skill and mental gymnastics with people thousands of miles away, for whom we will never know or even be interested in their name, gender, or nationality.

When will the metaverse happen?

Matthew Ball, metaverse expert, argues it will be at least 2026 before anything resembling a united interactive, participatory, virtual internet will look anything like the sci-fi vision some of us have.

Others, like metaverse blogger and gamer Jon Radoff, argue we are already living in the metaverse, and it is developing rapidly. That school of thought says, just as no-one announced the birth of the internet, no-one will announce the launch day of the metaverse.

It will develop in fits and starts, slowly and then quickly, creeping upon us in good and less good ways. We won't even know when it has arrived, and by the time it does, we may well be on our way to Web 4.0, the meta-metaverse.

Many might assume the term 'metaverse' was invented by Mark Zuckerberg, the CEO of Facebook, along with his fellow visionaries at the largest internet company in the world. After all, on October 19, 2021, Mr Zuckerberg announced that the parent company of Facebook, which also owns WhatsApp, Instagram and the virtual reality hardware and software company Oculus, would change its name to Meta.

There followed days of interviews from the CEO, as well as his representatives, in the press, as well as a long multi-part video, released on the new Meta website. They announced that the company was changing to reflect the development of a 2D internet where people scrolled up and down screens, into a virtual space, where participants could be entirely immersed.

"I think this is a persistent, synchronous environment where we can be together, which I think is probably going to resemble some kind of hybrid between the social platforms that we see today, but an environment where you're embodied in it," Zuckerberg told TheVerge.

In technology, shared online space, communication, development of code, and gaming, goes back at least until 1978. And since the 1990s, internet and gaming companies have shown real interest in creating an all-encompassing virtual interactive world, in which players or actors can move around, transact, and more recently attend conferences and concerts in live time.

A key player in this space, for example, has been Epic Games, who own the online gaming platform Fortnite. Certainly, Fortnite already provides a number of the ideas and functions that most imagine the metaverse will feature: an online virtual presence accessible via specially made headsets, if you want to; the opportunity to 'world build' within the foundations of the world that Fortnite has already provided; shopping and exchanging goods using virtual money; attending gigs, concerts and meeting with friends within the game, as avatars designed and dressed by their own creators; and the opportunity for commercial interests, such as Nike, to promote their own goods and advertise to users within the platform.

Asked over Twitter in December 2020 if Fortnite was a game or a platform, CEO Tim Sweet of Epic Games, wrote: "Fortnite is a game... primarily. But with every update and every new creative map, it grows closer towards being a place and a platform. 2021 will be a very interesting year for this!" Pushed by his questioner, he replied: "I'll adhere to the 1990's definition that something is a platform when the majority of content people spend time with is created by others."

Thought the *idea* of the metaverse is nothing new, one idea that perhaps has not been posited as firmly before, but is now emerging is *interoperability*. Where previously companies, and individual creators, would create their own games, platforms, currencies, characters, and rules, the new metaverse suggests all of these work *together*. They will interact with each other, in an increasingly seamless way, to make a user feel they are in and using a singular metaverse, rather than continually logging in and out of different platforms.

That will only come about if the vision of large, established social media and technology companies work together with smaller creators, coders, entrepreneurs and more, and if every party is willing to *share* their platforms to create something that at least feels united for the user. The large and small internet companies that already exist, as well as those smaller entrepreneurs newly inspired by the opportunities the metaverse offers, will have to work together, share data, and most importantly share pathways in and out of each other's previously exclusive space.

The metaverse in that sense does not yet exist, and isn't even close. Nor do some of the other key aspects to the metaverse: cheap, accessible, and useable headsets, computer servers that can process that much data at a time, fast enough bandwidth in our home internet connections, hardware in our houses and workplaces.

Until the sharing of data becomes generalized, and the hardware required becomes widespread, the metaverse will not exist as current participants understand it.

As Matthew Ball puts it in his seminal essay: "The

metaverse will require countless new technologies, protocols, companies, innovations, and discoveries to work. And it won't directly come into existence; there will be no clean 'Before the metaverse' and 'After metaverse'. Instead, it will slowly emerge over time as different products, services and capabilities integrate and meld together."

Mark Zuckerberg told TheVerge: "I think a good vision for the metaverse is not one that a specific company builds, but it has to have the sense of interoperability and portability. You have your avatar and your digital goods, and you want to be able to teleport anywhere. You don't want to just be stuck with one company's stuff... the software that we build, for people to work in or hang out in and build these different worlds, that's going to go across everything." In the same interview, he acknowledges that even his own hardware - the Oculus series of headsets - are not sufficiently user friendly to be adequate portals into the metaverse. (They're heavy and a little cumbersome.)

The question as yet unanswered is whether the larger companies will attempt to build their own metaverses, enclosed by their own passwords and digital walls, which in a sense go to war with each other for dominance of the market. Or more likely, the large companies begin to work together more to create a single metaverse in which each benefit, and the consumer benefits too.

The near future is likely to answer that question.

A new sense of reality?

When we think about the metaverse, a vision of 3D bodies moving around in a room immediately springs to mind. But when that is drilled down, we're not always imagining the same thing. To help us along, here are a few definitions.

3D - Three dimensional. Experiencing something in three dimensions, as if it has real height, width, and depth. We experience 3D in real life. In computers, and on 3D images and optical illusions, our brains are tricked into experiencing 3D. One might add a fourth dimension of sound, and perhaps a fifth of touch, when it comes to the development of the metaverse. Smell and taste may also be on the long term agenda.

Augmented reality (AR) - The projection of computer generated reality onto a real-life experience. Augmented reality includes real life, and mixes it with computer generated imagery and experience. An easy example would be the projection of a hologram, which appears to exist in real space, but is in fact a trick of computer programming and light projection. A more complex example might be entering the metaverse to create a model of a building, then 3D printing that building in the real world. It went from a virtual idea into a real object. Another example is the use of AR glasses. We walk around a museum looking at objects in real life, but are fed a stream of information about what we're looking at on the glass lenses that only we can see. The experience of real life and virtual information is united.

Virtual reality (VR) - This involves completely entering into another world, currently by using a headset, and perhaps gloves and sensors. Virtual reality excludes the real world, so as to enhance the virtual experience. However, it is likely that the lines between virtual reality and real reality may be more blurred as the metaverse develops.

We may be able to shop in a virtual shop, seeing the products before us, and feel the weight of the products through our special gloves, as we move them from the virtual shelves into our virtual shopping trolley.

We may be able to meet our work colleagues virtually, see them (or more likely their avatar), hold our hand out, squeeze their hand, feel them squeezing ours, then turn to screens in the virtual world and feel marker pens in our hand, which we can use to draw diagrams, or manipulate information.

We're not there yet.

As Zuckerberg acknowledges, headsets are not in that place right now. Anyone who has tried a virtual reality headset, may likely have experienced their weight, the sometimes 'cartoony' and blocky effect of the visuals, the slightly stilted interaction. Virtual headsets are good at showing us stuff, but they are far from good at making us feel we are in the world we're seeing, and much less acting inside it.

For the time being, participating in the virtual world is one of being on the outside looking in, rather than a virtually immersive experience. But developments are apace. The metaverse is likely to feature us pulling on gloves, perhaps even suits, so that our physical movements can be tracked and transferred into the virtual world. In later developments, the gloves we wear are likely to be able to measure how hard we grasp something, and transfer that information to virtual experience. On the flip side, our experience in the virtual world - that of shaking hands for example - is likely to be mirrored in the real world using pressure sensors in the gloves. We will feel the real experience of shaking hands, not just see it in virtual.

This kind of technology does already exist, but only at high research levels. A few sets of gloves and sensors, used by scientists in universities and research labs. It's clunky and unrealistic, often designed with one specific task or operation in mind.

Transferring this specialist equipment to the commercial, and then into the affordable for every household, may be the biggest test the metaverse has to face. Consumers are going to want to buy and use this stuff, so the general public may need convincing it is worth it.

It is important to say that most commentators do not define the metaverse as entirely a virtual reality experience. Instead, they regard it as just one part of what the internet will look like in ten to fifteen years time.

We will still, for example, be able to deal in entirely virtual currency that exists only in the metaverse, without having to pull on a headset to shake hands with a meta-coins trader.

We will be able to attend a virtual meeting with our work colleagues just as we do now, via our computer screens and cameras, without having to adorn some kind of digital avatar costume. It's just that some of the colleagues we're talking to might be wearing their avatars when we talk to them. We will still be able to view goods entirely created in the metaverse, buy them with Metacoin, and store them in our own personal metaverse locker or house, without virtually stepping into the metaverse ourselves.

Take aways

- The history of the metaverse is one of continual technological advancement, not one-time inventions.
- Mark Zuckerberg launched a whole new era of

speculation about the metaverse when the parent company of Facebook renamed itself Meta on October 18, 2021.

- The idea of the metaverse is nothing new. The term 'metaverse' first appeared in the 1994 sci-fi novel *Snow Crash* by Neil Stephenson, but ideas go back even further.
- The metaverse envisages a world where various platforms, online and offline, 2D, 3D and virtual work together.
- The metaverse will require countless new technologies not yet invented to become what its proponents are suggesting it will be.

THE METAVERSE NOW

Jon Radoff, a keen advocate of the metaverse, and commentator on all things gaming and technical, identifies some of the key attributes we can expect from the metaverse. The ideas and titles are his, the attempt at explanations are mine.[1]

Eye tracking - your headset will track your eye pupils, and what you see in the virtual world will reflect where you are actually looking, not just where your head is pointing;

Smart glasses and headsets - these will range from glasses you wear day to day in your real life, which may have a stream of data, such as a Facebook feed, running in a corner where you can focus; to headsets that encompass all of your eyes, cutting out the outside world and subjecting you wholly to the virtual world;

Location aware maps - think Google maps, continuously updated depending on your actual position, and available in the virtual space, as well as through your smart glasses when not in the virtual world. You may be able to virtually 'jump' to any location on the planet, and see what is there (depicted like Google Street does now) or a virtual version of it. You will also be able to do the same inside the virtual world;

Holographic - 3D images you can see and interact with through your smart glasses in the real world, as well in the virtual world. May be renders of friends and colleagues, but just as likely to be strangers, robots, inanimate objects or something as yet unthought of;

Open source - the process where anyone can take the code behind a computer program or virtual world, edit it, add to it, and develop it to create something new, or a better version of what currently exists. Wikipedia is an open source encyclopedia. OpenOffice is a suite of open source applications featuring a word processor, spreadsheet program and a presentation App. In the metaverse, it is likely that anyone will be able to develop aspects of the new internet, either from raw code, or on platforms specifically created to do it;

Avatars - online representations a user of the metaverse, created by the user. To date, this has involved users being offered 'skins', including costumes, appearance, facial and body changes, movement and accessories. In battle games, avatars might include the equipment like weapons you have won, paid for, or stolen. In sports games, avatars might feature a personally designed kit, a persona you've taken on such as a real world footballer, or a particular set of skills you've earned;

Virtual beings - the metaverse may feature non-human beings created by software designers, to carry out certain tasks, such as serving your avatar's needs, but just as likely to prevent your avatar from achieving their goals, or even committing some kind of virtual crime like stealing your online currency;

Artificial intelligent (AI) beings - these will be non-human, computer generated and controlled beings, programmed to learn from the human avatars and the situations around them. They may be strictly controlled, or let loose to learn and build for themselves;

Speech and language recognition - the metaverse is likely to learn to recognize words and linguistics in general, and the particular language and intonations of particular users, in order to better respond to our needs. Translation will be far more accurate than even current artificial intelligence efforts, resulting in the ability to seamlessly communicate with other avatars who you do not share a language with;

Visual recognition - your headset, glasses, tablet and virtual system will automatically identify you as a user, and you will be able to 'plug' into the metaverse from wherever you are, without needing your own particular hardware - such as at a hotel, or on a bus;

Brain/computer interface - it is already possible to create movements on a computer screen through thoughts alone, through computer recognition of brain electronic patterns. Expect this to develop alongside the metaverse, resulting in the likely control of our avatars by thoughts or concentration, or by thinking about a problem and being presented with the solution;

Simulation - the huge power of the servers and memory behind the metaverse, as well as the multi-mind resources created by it, will enable large and accurate computer models to be created of everything from climate change, to moves to tackle poverty, to try out different democratic scenarios, project and predict business sales, and rapidly test ideas, plans and predict markets for new products;

Supply chain, logistics, manufacturing - more accurate models, as well as the ongoing live and updating response of users, buyers, sellers, traders, and shareholders, alongside weather projections and monitoring, will enable yet more seamless supply chains for goods, that will be better at predicting future blockages in supply and demand;

Constantly learning - through artificial intelligence, constantly monitoring and testing, and through continuous feedback, the metaverse might be able to sense and adjust to create the best of possible metaverses in any particular time and scenario. Likewise, users of the metaverse will be constantly learning and gaining from the wider access to information, and participation in what the metaverse has to offer;

Smart homes to smart cities - sharing and modelling, alongside sound artificial intelligence, will lead to proposed solutions to some of our problems. Traffic issues, carbon emissions, communications, and more will be tested in the metaverse, then rolled out into the real world if deemed effective. Our homes, streets, places of work and leisure will be seamlessly connected to the metaverse, responding to our environment and behavior, such as counting our steps, monitoring our eating habits, our risk taking levels, and reflecting them in the metaverse, perhaps along with advice and offering lessons to improve our lives;

3D worlds - More and more of our online life will be experienced as a 3D environment, with expectations that holograms, 3D images, films and design tools will be 3D generated. 2D will feel as outdated as black and white movies;

Virtual world - There will be an opportunity to access most of our lives wholly online, in a fully virtual world, from learning, working and earning, to socializing, gaming, exercise, and spending;

Virtual economies - there will be currencies and

economies that exist entirely within the metaverse, which will have no value outside the metaverse but are significant. We will be able to earn, spend, and gain interest on our virtual currency, and invest it in objects that exist only in the metaverse. However, we will also be able to put real money into the metaverse, by buying up virtual currency, or selling virtual currency, to earn real money;

Sports and games - we're likely to see the computer games we currently play online unite under a single accessible platform, and for scores, medals, currency and branding, items, sponsorship and our avatars to be transferable between games; we will be able to carry out virtual versions of our favorite sports, but also use trackers on our body when playing sport in the real world, to transfer that data to the metaverse, in order to analyze our exercise, or even replay a sport we've done and learn to improve our technique;

Teams, clans, leagues, groups - we are likely to see every kind of interest group represented in the metaverse, sometimes drilled down to specific categories. Groups will be able to chat, share, celebrate, socialize and carry out their tasks in the metaverse. Where a team or group does not have the functionality to carry out a task online, they are likely to be able to commission that work to be carried out, creating a new asset that could then be shared with similar groups, or sold for profit;

Creator economy and creator platforms - the metaverse is likely to foster open and closed source creation of new ideas, art, music, film, and assets as yet unthought of, which can be created and shared or sold. Creators might work at any number of levels: from raw coding of the metaverse, to platforms created to enable creators to do basic programming to create games; to platforms which have boundaries for convenience, but allow creators to work within them, such as the online design program Canva, or a garden design program, or the drag and drop web design platforms like WordPress;

Opportunities to make money - from the outside, the metaverse will offer opportunities for investors to buy shares in companies building the future of the internet, or developing aspects within it, as well as for small companies and entrepreneurs who have something to offer the development and improvement of the platform. But there will also be opportunities, as there already are, for users of the metaverse to invest, buy and sell digital assets in the metaverse, and to create something new in the metaverse which they can then go on to sell and make real money from;

Community chat rooms and platforms - chat in public and in private online spaces are likely to be a key aspect of the metaverse. Users will be able to communicate directly, in all the ways we have become used to in real time: voice, video, messaging, video messaging, Tweeting, image sharing, news feeds, blogs, discussion forums, attend concerts and events, and share emojis. But there is likely to be a growth in group meetings and events, and a move away from physically moving from home, to office, to social space, to gym, to place of historic importance;

Immersive entertainment - we will be able to travel, attend music events, enjoy movies and theatre with others in the virtual space, without leaving home - if that is what we wish. With developed virtual reality and tools, those spaces and experiences may feel almost as real as attending an event or place in person and will certainly be more accessible and cheaper;

Work - almost all aspects of non-physical work will be

able to be carried out in the metaverse, from meeting with colleagues in person via our avatars, sharing data and documents we have created; to teaching, training, creating, designing, and testing ideas. The metaverse will create a swathe of new jobs, not only coding and platform designing, but virtual architects, independent creators and artists in the virtual space, planners, legislators, celebrities, entrepreneurs, and its own brand of fat cats there only to make cash. The metaverse may also provide opportunities to design, model and test ideas for new modes of work in the real world, influencing how labor, manufacture, and even economies are designed and rolled out.

I cover some of the above in more detail later in the book. It is sufficient to realize that there is not much in our lives that will not in some way be affected by the metaverse, just as the internet and mobile communications runs through every aspect of our current existence in the higher income world.

The metaverse in popular culture

If the metaverse seems all too familiar to you, that's probably because it is. The idea is not a new one, and you don't have to look far to see the ideas of virtual reality, 3D, computer generated life and virtual life in the popular culture we consume.

Commentators may credit Neil Stephenson's sci-fi adventure *Snow Crash* with invention of the term metaverse, but the idea of logic and computer generated worlds goes far further back than its publication in 1992.

Of course, there is the medium of gaming itself, which I have separated into a different section because of its significance. The following covers the other main elements of the metaverse reflected in popular culture.

Snow Crash

Unkindly, commentators have said this book is required reading in Silicon Valley, and that no-one interested in the future of the internet can speak authoritatively without reading it. The truth is that Neil Stephenson's 1992 futurist book is brilliantly written, and deserves to be read in its own right, not just because it was the first novel to use the word metaverse.

In the novel, the metaverse is an urban platform mirroring a road circulating its own world, which can only be accessed through a VR headset or through public telephone-like portals owned by a single company. Real estate around the virtual world can be purchased from its owner company, developed upon, and resold.

The metaverse exists continuously, while most interaction occurs between avatars designed by its users. There is an equivalent of currency, self-building of properties, a platform for viewing any place anywhere in world (this was pre-Google earth and Google maps), avatars, entirely metaverse-created virtual reality assistants, and even an unlimited library made up of all the information anyone can stuff into it, and retrieve from it.

The action takes place in and without the metaverse in the novel, which posits a future of corporate monopolies owning what's left of a wrecked world.

Choose your own adventure

I remember this series of 'gaming' novels, published by Bantam Books from 1979, where the reader followed the main character, and at many points in each book, decided where the story should lead by turning to a particular page. The books spread across historical, Western, outer space, spy, and mystery worlds.

Each boasted 40 possible endings, with numerous ways to get there. The ones I read contained illustrations as well as text. Around the same time, text only based computer games were emerging, like the choose your own adventure version of *Hitchhikers Guide to the Galaxy*.

Though neither of these can be said to be anything close to the virtual reality of the metaverse, they both introduce deep user involvement in stories and adventure, rather than experiencing the passive reception of entertainment.

Metaverse commentator Jon Radoff adds to this list other books that, one way or another, touch on the elements of the metaverse such as 3D, virtual reality, alternative societies, and online training. They include various books by Vernier Verge, the futuristic novel *Daemon*, by Daniel Suarez, which includes a massive multiplayer online game; William Gibson's *Neuromancer*, and *Lexicon* by Max Barry.

He goes on further, to include a series of books by Ian M. Banks, ever the author of sleek futuristic challenging books.

My own short fiction book, *Future Shop,* tackles the idea of virtual worlds, and the benefits and negatives of becoming involved in them, as well as the challenge of - when virtual reality become the norm for all of us - distinguishing real experience from the digital. My book *Portico* examines the challenges of social media and corporate hacking on truth and real world politics.

Ready Player One (book and then film)

In this 2011 sci-fi fantasy novel by Ernest Cline, and the 2017 film adaptation by Stephen Spielberg, most of the plot takes place in a 2045 enclosed virtual platform called OASIS. It's a virtual world accessible through headsets, and is the only escape from drudgery for Wade Watts, the film's central character. Watts seeks out a hidden 'easter egg' - a secret treasure of some kind - hidden in the virtual world by its designer James Halliday. The finder of the easter egg will inherit Halliday's fortune and rights to the game.

Naturally, there are high resolution super-graphic car chases, fights, gunfights, virtual soldiers, and impossibly compelling gymnastics, and as we're getting to know from the metaverse now - real life and virtual life interchange at times, having severe effects on each other.

The key difference between the OASIS, it's argued, is that the virtual world described in Ready Player One is owned and run by a single profit making corporation, while our own future metaverse is likely to be something designed and owned by a number of companies, large or small, or perhaps by all its users, where any participants can design, build, participate and profit from the world we have all created.

Total Recall (1990)

Undoubtedly, one of the best early action movies to use the ideas of virtual reality to scare its audiences. Arnold Schwarzenegger, a manual laborer on a futuristic earth, has an unsatisfied urge to go to Mars. Unable to do so, he decides to take a 'virtual reality holiday experience' as a spy working on Mars, but from the moment the process is underway, Arnie gets paranoid and angry, and it's unclear whether the characters around him are part of his virtual spy thriller experience, or they are for real. Within his experience, he's invited to swallow a red pill that is a 'symbol' to end his dream and bring him back to his real body. This is widely regarded as a precursor to the red pill/blue pill scene in The Matrix.

The Matrix (1999)

Widely credited as the first credible and genuinely awe inspiring attempt to get into a possible reality of the computerized future. This 1999 science fiction film directed by Lana and Lilly Wachowski outdid its competitors not only in its 3D-like design, but the ideas it featured. It's as close, perhaps, as the metaverse might have been envisaged back then.

The Keanu Reeves vehicle contained all the sleek aspects of a traditional futuristic action movie - excellent fight scenes, long leather jackets, super slick weaponry, acrobatics and, of course, cool shades - but not too long into the film, Reeves' character Neo learns the truth about his existence: that he only actually exists, consciously, in The Matrix. Duly, his brain is fed a 'real life experience' which is nothing of the sort, but it keeps him and thousands upon thousands of other humans docile, so that aliens can power their own lifestyles by harvesting the energy humans produce. He symbolically takes the red pill (the truth) rather than the blue (the existing reality) to discover what's really going on.

Neo is brought out of the energy harvesting by a resistance movement. Once aware of his status as 'the one' (Neo, get it!) has to fight for independence by re-entering the

Matrix and tackling the virtual reality bad guys the Matrix creates to defend itself.

Phew!

But the premise works, and only now can we see something similar emerging for our own futures. Sure, the social media and new technology companies won't be harvesting our actual energy, but we may likely be giving a modern day matrix our personal data, our money, our attention, and our own time and contribution to its building and development.

The metaverse is likely to be so pervasive, in the higher income world at least, that it may be hard to exist without participating in some form, and there's every chance that in one way or another, we will be compelled to contribute. After Covid-19, I can't re-order a medical prescription without going online, logging into my health service account, and ticking boxes. Okay, I don't go in with a slow-mo flying kick or a tumble through the air, but the days of calling into the doctor's surgery to ask for a repeat are long gone.

Minority Report (2002)

The 2002 Stephen Spielberg futuristic action movie, starring Tom Cruise, posits a world where crime perpetrators are arrested before they've actually committed the crime. It also features a kind of viewing experience and interactive experience for the protagonist that cannot be far away from what using and experiencing the metaverse might look like.

The pre-recognition of the murderer is based on data and instinct of character, held in the interaction between three supernaturally intelligent beings, but also their interaction with datasets held on computers. To understand, track down, and plan his missions to take down the pre-criminals, Cruise uses a futuristic surround screen full of holograms. He manipulates the images and holograms on screen, with special gloves which he uses to swipe images away, pull holograms into better view, expand and retract what he's seeing, and scroll through timelines and news articles.

As an added touch, the film is peppered with futuristic ideas like a newspaper that continually updates itself (not too far away from our own current newsfeeds), an idea also shown in Paul Verhoeven's Total Recall, which Minority Report was first considered a sequel too.

Wreck it Ralph (2012) and Ralph Breaks the Internet (2019)

These children's animated films feature the arcade game character from Fix-It Felix Jr, a real life 2014 pixelated computer game. The film is based on the idea that gaming characters can act independently in their games, and as the plots develop, enter into each other's games to accidentally 'wreck' and fix them. In Ralph Breaks The Internet, the main character enters 'the internet' as a whole, and is presented with various buildings and operations, labelled by the brands we know well: Amazon, Google, Netflix, and the games many of us will be familiar with like Fortnite, Pac-Man and Street Fighter. There are cameos for lots of Disney characters.

The value to kids is to see all of their favorite gaming, film and social media references playing off against each other in a harmless, fun movie. The value to adults is to see the possible future interaction between brands and functions that the metaverse is likely to embody.

Will we virtually walk up to a Google desk, and ask for a search, as the Google virtual assistant before us attempts to pre-guess what we are searching for? Will we virtually browse goods on eBay, then enter an auction to buy what we want by raising our avatar's virtual hand, then pay for the goods in virtual currency?

Or for that matter, will we virtually walk through the metaverse and not be able to go far without seeing virtual kittens doing silly faces, or virtual cute babies, or somebody's avatar doing the floss?

Black Mirror

Charlie Brooker, the British writer, commentator, and comedian is behind this ground-breaking five part series of 'what if' scary futuristic one hour films. Many of the films take apart a certain aspect of currently consumed online media - online 'likes', online dating, privacy and access to data, celebrity, memory, identity, living online - and subjects it to the powerful medium of story to illustrate its benefits and danger points. The Black Mirror of the title signifies the cracked screen of our mobile devices.

Three particular Black Mirror episodes stand out as being way beyond their time, originally broadcast in 2018 to 2020, when we now look at the emergence of the metaverse.

In 15 Million Merits, Brooker posits a world of individuals living in some kind of prison, in which their only job is seemingly to power the existence of the building they are captured in. Each participant lives in a virtual world where their bedroom walls are made up of glass panels advertising porn and entertainment, and information they don't quite want to see.

When they workout on static bicycles, they earn 'merits', which they can spend on food and on opportunities - the most desirable of these being entry into a talent competition called Hot Shots that might allow them to be free of the endless universe they are trapped in. Hot Shots is run by three freaky characters, all too familiar as judges of well-known real life TV talent shows, while the audience is made up of avatars of those not yet selected for the game, who cheer and clap.

In Nosedive, the characters are forever on their mobile screens, linked up with retinal implants, and every interaction they have with each other is quietly rated. People spend more time looking into their screens than at each other's faces, and the rest of the time they spend creating and perfecting their own face and appearance, so that it looks good to other viewers, so they rate them highly.

The result is an aggressive fake happiness, where users try to outdo each other in their cheeriness and perfection, so as to continue to score highly with their ratings. The main character, Lacie, has her eyes on her perfect home, and the real estate agent tells her she can have it at an affordable 20% discount if she can keep her rating about 4.5. The story follows her desperate attempts to raise her rating, which in turn often leads to reduced rating as she's trying too hard, or realizes she can't please all the people all the time.

What Brooker and his writers are doing here is positing a world where we create a fake persona to please and gain traction with every other fake persona, in order to achieve certain goals. It is very easy to see how such ideas could transition to the metaverse, where everyone has an avatar, the desire to be seen as their perfect self, and to earn, build and live so as to impress other avatars.

A posited future, where the metaverse and our real life are not separated, but intimately integrated, offers a stark warning about what the future might bring.

In Bandersnatch, Brooker takes the world of virtual media to another level, actually asking the person watching the film to interact with the film itself. The watcher selects what the main character should do at specific plot points, and the film goes down different paths depending on the selection, and finishes in a different place as a result of decisions made.

It is just like the old Choose Your Own Adventure books (referenced in the film), or their online text-based equivalents that made up some of the earlier computer games. Because of the limits of our technology in 2018, Bandersnatch felt a little clunky, and it was easy to go back, try out a different path, and by the end of the film, you'd pretty much tried out all the scenarios. But there were very clever and funny parts too, like when the character (based in 1988) claims he's being controlled by a futuristic entertainment platform called Netflix, in the 21st Century.

In the future, with the intervention of AI, as well as huge numbers of ongoing contributors making new pathways, story arcs, scenes and even characters, the same film in the metaverse might offer an entirely different experience for every single viewer of a film like Bandersnatch.

The 2018 film depended on a single person watching the film on a computer or interactive TV. It was not something you could engage with passively, with someone else, or at the cinema. The metaverse is very likely to open up the possibilities that Brooker plays with.

. . .

What all of these books and films share is that they are playing with ideas of what the future metaverse might look like, based on the technology we have today - or that were around at the time of writing. As well as trialling completely new ideas, many of them take what currently exists and attempts to push it further along, asking 'what next?'

That can be a benefit, but it also shows our weaknesses in predicting the future. In *Snow Crash*, which was written over 20 years ago, it was difficult for the writer to envisage a world where one could access the metaverse without having to have some kind of physical plug into it. Today, of course, we're so used to wireless communications that it doesn't occur to us to plug into anything.

In The Matrix, Neo had to have a physical implant in his neck, in order to re-enter the virtual world. His colleagues watched him on green and black screens, interpreting dropping rows of code to decipher Neo's actions. Why not just watch what he's doing through a headset and movie-like virtual 3D rendering?

From Dr Who in the sixties right through to movies like Star Wars, Wall-E, Short Circuit, Terminator, and iRobot, we struggle to consider the idea of a robot that is not in the shape of a human being, anthropomorphized into our very inefficient and unstable shape. While the droid R2-D2 in Star Wars was a cylinder on wheels, Ridley Scott gave the robot human emotions.

The truth is that the most effective and efficient robots are simply boxy hunks of metal, their parts interfacing with each other with pulleys, bearings, and levers, continuing their factory work effortlessly with no emotion, personality, or human features. Some factory workers even give those machines names, and stick on fake eyes, to make themselves more comfortable.

How far will the metaverse mirror these trends? We as yet do not know what the 'bots' and automations and virtual reality worlds of the metaverse will look like, and we must allow for a certain amount of the 'known unknowns' as we look to the future.

But this also raises the question of how far we will expect the metaverse to mirror human experience, or our interpretation of what a future human experience should look like, for it to be useable and comfortable for humans to live with.

The metaverse and gaming

Choose Your Own Adventure

I have already touched on what could arguably be called the first gaming dip in the ocean of the metaverse. As well as in books, you could play text based Choose Your Own Adventure games on your computer as far back as the 1970s.

Looking back, they don't seem so impressive. They were written in very basic code (often in a code known as BASIC), and the possibilities one could explore ran into two or three options at a time. Interaction with the game was minimum - 'look', 'go forward' - and the games could not react to their players. They could only take them down pre-determined tracks.

Nevertheless, the gamer was made to feel they were entering a separate world, in which they had some agency. Early visual games, like *Tennis* or *Frogger*, were external: the character on the screen reacted to what you did on the keyboard, but there was no feeling you were actually playing tennis, nor a frog trying to cross roads or streams.

In Choose Your Own Adventure, we at least felt some investment because we had intelligent choices to make. It was more judgement, than skill.

It can be argued, therefore, that the predecessors of the metaverse in the games world should be regarded as personally immersive, where the gamers interact more intimately with the game, or indeed with other players.

Command & Conquer (1994)

Command & Conquer as well as Command & Conquer: Red Alert, became the most popular early games that included real time sequences rather than players taking it in turns. Players could interact with each other, in an ongoing real time battle. Though the games were essentially 2D, with players looking down on a map illustrating the territory they'd won or lost, they could be played across the world with other gamers you didn't know. The game connected directly; it did not require an internet browser.

Total Annihilation (1997)

Refining the concept of Command & Conquer, building on the increased stability of internet connections, it allowed 3D terrain, weapons, and tanks. Though it was more strategic, players still didn't participate as avatars. Not long after, there was a rapid development of games in which players could move up, down and in 360 degrees, rather than just forward and backwards on a relatively flat surface.

These war and strategy type games were the precursors to fully fledged 3D generated experiences, but they were still games in which players won, lost, drew, or just got bored with the limited repetitive play. For things to move on - particularly away from the nerdy image of boys in their boxer shorts, sitting in a basement playing on their computers - gaming needed to expand its horizons. It needed to offer more than the slim choice between guns, ammo, cars for racing, or choice of a limited number of kung-fu characters like those Street Fighter II offered. Massively multiplayer online role-playing games (MMORG) were born.

Second Life (2003)

Though its developers, Linden Lab, said the platform was not a game, "there is no manufactured conflict, no set objective", Second Life is widely regarded as the precursor to all avatar-based online experiences. It offered users the opportunity to literally create a second life in a 3D world. Users could create avatars of their choosing, and could interact with other users, places, locations, and build, create, shop, and trade. The universe has its own currency, the Linden Dollar, which is exchangeable with real world currency.

Perhaps with a view towards what was to come, in September 2006, former Governor of Virginia Mark Warner became the first politician to appear in a virtual reality world when he gave a speech in Second Life. The band Redzone is said to be the first band to tour in Second Life in February 2007. In June 2008, author Charles Stross held a conference in Second Life to promote an upcoming novel.

Minecraft (2011)

This simple world building game, officially launched in 2011 but rolled out many years before, was so popular it easily broke out of the 3D world, and has become an offline brand too, with T-shirts, pencil cases, Christmas jumpers, mugs, watches and, ironically, real world board games and real world conventions.

In the game, which consists of blocks, players can create pretty much anything of their choosing in their own Minecraft world, or one which they share with other users in an infinite online space. Users can mine for raw materials, then use the materials or exchange them, to build anything from a boat to a castle; a river to a road.

While it seems a step back from Second Life, its sheer simplicity for kids and the harp back to something a little more mission based (I will build this castle, then invite others to visit it) has made it the biggest selling video game of all time.

Significantly, Minecraft users can design their own games in the platform, which other users can play, obeying the rules of the game set by its creators. This user-created aspect of gaming is likely to be a foundation of gaming in the metaverse, as well as for many other aspects of the future internet.

Fortnite (2017)

As already discussed above, the CEO of Epic Games which runs Fortnite has so far said Fortnite is not a platform, it is a game. But it does look more and more like a platform, with even my own kids complaining 'people just hang out in it, and they only give you a limited choice of guns'. Whatever its owners say, Fortnite has been ahead of the curve in creating what many suggest the metaverse will look like. In fact, commentators such as Gene Park in the Washington Post called Fortnite the first real metaverse company in April 2001, a full nineteen months before Facebook (now Meta) publicly declared its interest as a metaverse company.

A look at the game shows how easy the transition could be.

At first glance, Fortnite is a virtual reality battle game, in which you can choose your avatar, weapons, battle strategy and link up with other users online for the very high resolution game play in an infinite virtual universe.

Depending on which version you use, you can link with up to 100 other players at a time. Current hardware and software limitations prevent anything larger, though as the metaverse develops, Fortnite's capacity to host more players in one virtual world may increase too.

Players can pimp their avatars and their weapons by spending V-Bucks they earn in the game, or which they can buy with real world currency. In one form of the game, Fortnite creative, players can create their own games within the platform, such as battle arenas, challenges, and races.

Like in a future metaverse, brands can buy virtual space in Fortnite to display advertising, sponsor events and create their own games and promotional experiences. This tendency is what is taking the platform slowly further away from a gaming space, and into somewhere more social and experiential.

Famously, acts including Travis Scott, Marshmello, Jason Momoa, Drake, and Major Lazer have appeared at concerts to thousands live in Fortnite.

Roblox (2006)

This game playing and creation platform grew slowly, taking hold in 2010, but came into its own in 2020 during the Covid-19 outbreak, where young people turned online in masses for information and leisure. In August 2020, it had 164 million users worldwide - half of them under 16.

Like some of the other platforms, it has an online currency and the ability to play a range of games. Its users can code things for themselves using the platform, creating completely new games for others to play.

Those games don't have to be based in a Roblox virtual reality world. It is more like an App store, where freelancers can create games and Apps, then sell them (or most often offer them for free) to play through the Roblox marketplace. The result is thousands upon thousands of games, of varying degrees of quality, aimed at many different audiences.

Profits from purchases of games by users - as well as 'in-game' purchases - are shared between Roblox and the game designer. Users can also spend on Roblox to buy and create their avatar on the platform. The platform has also been used by bands, to perform concerts during the Covid-19 epidemic. More interesting, given its target age group, Roblox birthday parties - within the platform - became a big thing during the pandemic.

The particular challenge for Roblox has been its voice and message system, which is more stark because of its younger users. The platform has thousands of staff charged with seeking out and deleting offensive, predatory, sexual, and bullying materials, but not everything is caught.

Play to earn

YouTube has already given some expert gamers a lucrative form of income. Simply put, some players sit in front of their computer screens, and record their game play live, streaming it via YouTube. They get hundreds of thousands of followers, which YouTube harvests for data. Then goes on to deliver appropriate advertising.

The next logical step will be for this gaming to be taken into the metaverse. Brands like Red Bull and burger chain Wendy's have already made significant investment in virtual worlds, hosting, sponsoring or even designing virtual games themselves, with participants from all over the world.

It is very likely we may pay to attend gaming events in the metaverse, pay to participate, and we'll view advertising in those metaverse games, just like we do in real life. And if we're skilled enough to be a fantastic gamer, there's every chance we could walk away with hundreds of thousands of metaverse currency. Which we will then go on to spend in and out of the metaverse, building our own brand. As you'll see later, Play to Earn gaming is not just a quirky phenomenon, it is a full time job for some kids in the lower and middle-income world.

Take aways

- There is little in our lives that will not be affected in some way by the metaverse, just as the internet and mobile communications run through every aspect of our lives.
- Choose Your Own Adventure books were an

early form of metaverse, and later similar text-based computer games.

- Films in the 1990s played with the ideas around the metaverse, including Terminator, The Matrix and Minority Report.
- Computer gaming has had a significant impact on our vision of what the metaverse is, and gaming will be the foundation of what the metaverse will become.
- Massively multiplayer online role-playing games (MMORG), such as Second Life, Minecraft and Fortnite, are arguably the first iteration of online metaverses.

WHAT HARDWARE WILL YOU NEED?

In The Matrix, Neo required a plug-in, in the back of his neck. In Neil Stephenson's *Snow Crash*, the main character Hiro Protagonist accesses the metaverse though goggles with fibre optic cables running down a plastic tube, or else via public booths which can only render their users in grainy black and white. In Charlie Brooker's Black Mirror, most interactions with the social media and communications world are through brain and retinal implants, or else special lenses.

How far these ideas are predictive of the metaverse is yet to be seen, but some of them do already exist and are likely to be at least the foundations of what we are likely to use in the future.

Internet connection

This might seem obvious, especially since you are most likely to have heard about this book online, and probably even bought it there. The metaverse requires a decent online connection, either through cabling or through mobile connection such as 5G and its future improvements.

A key limitation to users of the metaverse will be people's current inability to connect and participate in real time. The occasional, or even frequent, spinning wheel that indicates your web browser is waiting for information is something we all still experience. This indicates a slow internet connection, and definitely one too slow to do anything meaningful in the metaverse. However technologically advanced, amazing to look at and enjoyable the metaverse platforms are, they will not survive if most of the population don't have the bandwidth necessary to experience it in all its glory.

Note too, that when we talk about broadband speeds, we have to make the distinction between plugging our computers into a high speed network using an ethernet cable, compared with using a Wi-Fi signal. Using a direct cable is far more stable and faster than Wi-Fi, but will depend on its users being relatively static because their device is physically attached to a cable.

One can't help suspect being chained to the wall isn't what the authors of the metaverse are hoping for. But Wi-Fi and mobile communications present limitations too. They can be unstable. Slow, depending on how many users are accessing it in a house or office. And depending on how far a user is from the Wi-Fi unit, or whether they're behind a concrete wall or in a 'dead zone'

There is a fable in technological advance known as 'Moore's law' which posits that, in simple terms, the power of communications technology will double every two years. It is certainly possible that the development of the metaverse will outpace our ability to access it in its full form, because the coding of virtual technology may be developed faster than the roll out of the physical infrastructure needed to access it.

Infrastructure is boring. Virtual worlds, where virtual money can be exchanged, are not. If one doesn't keep pace with the other, we're likely to feel cheated and disenfranchised.

We won't be the first.

When Pew Research Center began systematically tracking Americans' internet usage in early 2000, about half of all adults were already online. Today, 93% of American adults use the internet. That leaves some who don't want to use the internet, but many who simple don't have access. In the UK, 97% of the population have internet access. In Australia, 89%. Across Europe, 90%.

But those figures don't tell the whole story. For the metaverse to become a daily, effective, seamless part of our lives, it will need to be high-speed, immediately available, and consistent. Many families simply don't have that high grade internet access, or anything like it.

In the UK, 97% of households have fast broadband access: it is delivered through fibre optic cables to the nearest telephone junction box, then finally delivered through copper wiring of the old telephone system to the property. It can deliver over 26 Megabits per second of data. It sounds like a lot, but plug three members of your family into the metaverse, with all this constantly regenerating 3D images and masses of data, and it may come to a grinding halt.

As of November 2011, the UK coverage of broadband fibre cable directly to people's homes - possibly likely to be able to cope with the metaverse at up to one gigabits per second (that's 1,000 times faster than one megabit per second) - is just 28.4%.[1]

In the United States, the average internet speed in the whole country is just 42.86 megabits per second, nowhere near the 1 Gigabits the metaverse is likely to need.[2]

According to the Pew Research Centre, those most unlikely to have fast, reliable broadband, come from the poorest backgrounds in society. Particularly those from black backgrounds, and those living in rural settings.

In the lower and middle-income world, countries are not even close to parity with the higher income world. In fact, mobile/smart phone communications over 4G signals far outstrips any broadband access across Africa and Asia (see below). Currently, that will limit users access to an emerging metaverse unless it is specifically designed to encompass mobile communications as it develops, and has the physical infrastructure to improve 4G and 5G signalling.

Mobile internet connection

Most of us already have our own cell phone or smartphone, and our kids do too. Meta is putting the mobile device above laptops and gaming consoles in its plans, so it seems clear they will play a large role. Not surprising when you look at the stats.

According to research collated by TechJury, up to 70% of web traffic comes from mobile devices, 95.1% of active Facebook traffic comes from mobile devices.

According to Statcounter, 47.59% of internet traffic is mobile and 48.88% is desktop, the rest from tablets. American adults spent four hours daily on their cell phones in 2020. This reflects a rise in 25% in 2021, compared with the year before.

Mobile phone usage for the internet is rising, despite it being half as fast as desktop access.

How can this fit into a metaverse which by its nature depends on speed, mobility and an all-encompassing experience?

In an article on Medium.com, Doug Antin argues that the metaverse already exists, in that we all use our mobile devices and smartphones to upload conversations, images, information, games and more. And we download the same, as well as concerts, music, books, and video interactions. And we can interact, through playing Fortnite or other online games, in real time.

He argues that to look at the metaverse as something that can only be accessed with special headsets in real time is to miss the point. Our own screens on smart phones offer us more than a window onto a virtual world, they are part of the metaverse themselves, and will continue to be into the future.

He reminds us that the mobile device presents our closest current experience of augmented reality: where data and images can be overlaid on top of real images in the real world. Take an App on a smart phone that tells us what stars we are pointing our camera at? Google Lens allows us to point our mobile phone camera at food, or plants, or buildings, and Google will tell us what we are looking at. We can look at a live-selfie image of ourselves, and add bunny ears or a Hallowe'en mask, take a photo, and upload it to our storage cloud.

"The bottom line is that you don't need to have a VR headset to interact with the metaverse. Regardless of your level of immersion, you can interact with the metaverse directly from a keyboard. Even adding a photo to Instagram counts," Antin writes.

In the lower and middle-income world, mobile device access to the internet far outweighs desktop and computer access. Africa has the highest mobile usage of the internet with 70%, while Asia came second with 63%. Compare that with Europe, which is the third biggest user of mobiles to access the web at just 51%.

If we are to experience a seamless experience of the metaverse, it is clear that technology for the platforms will have to be clearly steered towards our increasing usage of mobile smart devices (or future equivalents). But also, the infrastructure for delivering higher amounts and faster data to our mobile devices will be required too.

CEO of Meta, Mark Zuckerberg, told technology magazine TheVerge: "You can think about [the metaverse] as the successor to the mobile internet." But he doesn't explain how this is going to be squared with our increasing use of mobile devices, nor the lower and middle-income world's absolute reliance on them.

Fortune Daily writes: "Today's fourth-generation (4G) connections can just about support multiplayer Apps like Fortnite but can't handle hundreds of concurrent streams of time-sensitive data. This is why mobile carriers around the world are spending billions of dollars to build 5G networks. They may need even 6G to take it further."

Headsets, VR headsets and AR glasses

It is worth here quickly defining the difference between headsets, goggles, and glasses. In current parlance, a gaming or computer *headset* is a pair of headphones. They're usually decent ones that block out other sounds, along with a microphone so that users can converse with others in a game, or offer voice instructions to the platform they're engaged with. This type of headset is widely available.

A *VR headset* covers the eyes, and blocks out light from

outside. The 'virtual reality' experience is as close to virtual reality as it is currently able to achieve, with the user able to turn their head, and the picture before them moves accordingly. Meta's Oculus system, Samsung's Gear, Google's Daydream, and PlayStation all have serious investment in VR headsets and software.

AR glasses or *AR headsets* provide 'augmented reality', a half-and-half experience. The user can see the real world through them, but on the lens can also see data, images, even video to augment what the user is seeing through the glasses. Apple has been promising them for years but has yet to deliver. Facebook also sees them as a distant dream, working only currently on glasses with Ray-Ban that can take photos, and record audio and video.

When we think of the metaverse, we would most likely be thinking of VR headsets, and a wholly 3D experience. However, as we are learning throughout this book, the real vision of the metaverse is something quite different: with lots of access points, computer, mobile, glasses, even holograms, it will not be an experience only accessible through a particular headset.

What the everyday user will need will most likely depend on how immersed they want to be in the internet of tomorrow, as well as what they can afford, and developments of the hardware to make it more accessible and comfortable to wear.

As Zuckerberg admits to TheVerge: "Today, the VR headsets, they're still kind of a bit clunky, they may be a bit heavier than you would ideally like them to be. There needs to be advances in being able to express yourself and having higher resolution, being able to read text better, a number of things like that. But we're getting there, and each version is better and better."[3]

Games consoles

Arguably, games platforms like PlayStation, Xbox and Nintendo already give us a clear idea of what the metaverse might look like, and more and more games are being created that are best experienced while wearing VR headsets.

But even without the headsets, the pictures in FIFA, Fortnite and other high-resolution graphics presented on a large 2D screen can easily be mistaken for real, with a casual glance.

With such tech already in place, it is likely that consoles will play an ever increasing role in the internet of the future. The vision of the metaverse includes consoles, but also gloves. Both might give real-time feedback, as we use them to move around, browse and play in the metaverse. We might 'feel' products as we lift them, through pressure pads built into our gloves. Our consoles, as they do now, will rock and vibrate, when we move them, or crash, or steer. The vibrations and turning sensations we currently feel and use in our gaming consoles may become far more sophisticated.

However, there is work to do to make them compatible, and to sort out rights issues. For example, Roblox is available on Xbox, but not on PlayStation. Minecraft is available on all consoles, but only Minecraft Bedrock Edition can be played with others using a different system from your own. FIFA is currently non-cross platform, meaning those you are playing must be using the same console as you.

How far will this console-specific interaction problem proliferate into the metaverse space is yet to be seen. But it is likely to be an issue if games producers are not willing to share connections with each other.

Desktop computers, laptops, and tablets

It's almost too easy to forget about these. Like our mobile devices, we use them every day and they are a seamless gateway into the internet. At least at the beginning, we're likely to continue to use our computers to access the future internet, and the transition to VR headsets, mobile screens and other platforms is likely to be slow, simply because we're all so used to what we have been using since computers developed from circuit boards.

But it is worth some care here. I can touch type (without looking at the keys), and I use a tracker pad on my Mac. There was a time when I used a physical 'mouse' attached to my computer, and wouldn't have envisaged using a tracker pad. As time has gone by, my screen has become flatter and flatter. What I mean by a 'computer' now, is far from what I had when I was growing up. I'm so embarrassed by the world 'computer', I prefer to say Mac or laptop.

And when I look at my kids: they can't type like I can, but boy can they move around their phones, their Kindle Fires, and their school Chromebooks at speed, prodding screens and talking out loud to Alexa, Google, and Siri. And to my embarrassment, if I have a problem with my cell phone, I turn to them to help me solve it.

Perhaps we will continue to use some kind of computer in our own homes as the metaverse develops. It is yet to be clear what that technology will look like, or how many upgrades we will need to make in order to fully benefit from what will be on offer.

Gloves, motion detectors, cameras, lasers, and projectors

The more of this stuff we have, the more immersive the metaverse is likely to be. Imagine wearing a developed lightweight VR headset, a full immersion suit and gloves filled every few millimeters with microchips, being continuously read by a laser computer, which can then track our every move, gesture, our heart rate, our blood pressure, even our psychological state. Before us, we might be interacting with a 3D hologram of our friends' avatars, projected into our own kitchen by laser projectors placed around the walls.

All of these things currently exist and will develop and become less cumbersome into the future, and they will work together.

The technology is currently expensive, but it is likely to develop quickly. The likelihood of these things becoming mainstream is dependent only on our desire to have it (or the power of persuasion of those who have an interest in selling it to us).

As yet unknown

The beauty and challenge of the metaverse is that it is likely to contain elements we have not yet thought of, or don't think are realistic.

There will be applications, hardware, inventions, new programs and Apps that become popular and useful in the metaverse that we currently cannot even conceive of. Just like when I was a teenager, and had no idea computers would ever be able to communicate with each other by radiowaves (Bluetooth), or that I'd hold a phone in my hand

and use it to look up more information in a second, than was contained in the whole of our local library.

Take aways

- The development of the metaverse will require better integrated technology than we currently have, particularly faster broadband speeds.
- Much of metaverse engagement is likely to be via mobile devices, but connections are not yet strong or wide enough to do what is envisaged.
- A key component will be virtual reality headsets, and augmented reality glasses, with which we engage with virtual worlds in the metaverse.
- Gaming equipment is likely to improve and morph into equipment for the metaverse, but it will also require better compatibility between gaming platforms.
- Other hardware, such as sensory gloves, cameras and lasers will enable us to become more immersed in virtual worlds.

ARTIFICIAL INTELLIGENCE

In his *9 Megatrends Shaping the Metaverse*, commentator Jon Radoff argues that machine intelligence will be one of the vital ingredients for the internet of tomorrow.

"Computers will become collaborators in the creative process," he says. "We will transpose a life of looking at computers from the outside, to one of being inside the virtual world and it being all around us."[1]

He points out that many of the artificial intelligence (AI) trends we have come to see over the last ten years will come into their own in the near future, particularly in the metaverse where we will rely on computers to do basic work on our behalf.

Jon Radoff argues that in the metaverse, AI might play the following roles:

- Design and build microchips to process the information;
- Recognize and interpret human gestures;

- Predict and read eye movements and read emotions;
- Recognize the firing of brain neurons;
- Advise developers about their communications, integrations and where everything fits, and circumvent parts that don't fit;
- Will find and uncover the information we ask for;
- Will populate the virtual space itself.

Some commentators argue that AI will go further. That the many thousands of real life workers recruited to develop the metaverse, may in some senses be creating the artificial intelligence functions that will eventually replace them.

Though this might sound like the beginnings of self-awareness by artificial intelligence (I'm thinking Skynet in Terminator 2: Judgement Day here, see below), is it too far a jump?

We can easily imagine a gifted computer programmer designing artificial intelligence that can work as quickly and intelligently to build ever better versions of itself, testing itself perhaps in the metaverse, to continuously improve.

Jon Radoff says: "Some people say it will never happen. I think that's wishful thinking — there's no reason to believe machines won't be able to match or even surpass us."

At the very least, we can expect the AI we create for the metaverse to act in advisory roles for the improvement of metaverse technology, if not for their own improvement.

It seems certain that we are likely to experience artificial intelligence in the metaverse as something so present, we barely notice it. Just as we type a search into Google, we give no thought to the many thousands of processes the algorithms are going through not only to search for what we want, but to ensure its answers (and its advertising) are targeted directly to us: our age, gender, education, background, computer literacy and more. One person's Google search results screen is not the same as another's. That is artificial intelligence right there, we just don't call it that.

In the metaverse, we will receive exactly the same kind of tailored experience we have on Google. At the beginning of this book, I began with a scenario which included a toy shop. I invited you to imagine that as soon as you walked in, there were shelves packed with toys appropriate to your own children's ages.

> *"The shop already has a profile of you. It automatically shows you 3D projections of the toys most suitable for your family. No plastics, no fake guns... You call for 'soccer'. A whole shelf of soccer related toys hurtles towards you in 3D. You swipe a kid's soccer shirt. It appears, already in your daughter's size. A matching pair of shorts appear, though you didn't request them. Both go into a virtual shopping basket. An avatar (of a race and gender an algorithm has decided is most likely to ensure you complete the transaction) smiles as you swipe to pay."*

This is the same kind of algorithm as Google currently runs, but in a virtual world. It is artificial intelligence. The prediction of what you *might* want, based on what you have in the past, or on what others *like you* have bought in the past, starts to get unnerving. But it happens to us every day. And the metaverse will be full of it.

Popular culture traditionally makes us think about robots and AI in physical form (Terminator 1) and then in a more refined form (Terminator 2, iRobot), but there hasn't been much about what we can expect from a virtual artificial intelligence visually. This is perhaps because it is not necessary: we don't need to actually see an online robot or algorithm to understand it is at work.

However, since it might feel uncomfortable for us to be entirely within a virtual world by using VR headsets, we might actually *like* and be more comfortable if there was a virtual body for us to speak to - even if they represent an algorithm, or some other kind of AI we don't quite understand. Many still haven't got the hang of calling out Siri or Alexa if they want to search on iPhone or Amazon, and turn to their habit of using Google because they find it more comfortable and reliable.

A quasi-physical appearance for AI in the metaverse might not be necessary, but it might make users a whole lot more comfortable if we can see something.

What might be interesting is whether the companies behind the metaverse again decide to converge: *this* is what an artificial intelligence 'bot' should look like in the metaverse. Otherwise, won't we be seeing Facebook bots, Alexa bots, Siri bots and Google bots, and any other number of AIs in different forms, which may wear down trust?

But on the flipside, if every bot looks the same, might they be too easy to imitate by criminal hackers, and that might generate privacy and safety issues?

To conclude, it is important not to think of AI as some separate add-on to the future of the internet. It will be fully integrated, just as it is today. Only in a more developed form.

Facebook, in particular, is ploughing millions into research on creating real life looking automated avatars (using model humans, with sensors attached, to create real body shapes and movements), improving algorithms and AI, and creating its own 'Spark AR' platform that will allow independent developers to create their own AI programs and experiences.

In the metaverse, AI will be more powerful, offering better opportunities but also some new challenges.

Take aways

- Artificial intelligence will play a significant role in the metaverse, including in its design.
- AI may become so present in our lives, we will not notice it, just as we don't think about the algorithms running the platforms are used to.
- Commentators worry that AI might be too powerful in the metaverse.
- Though not required, we're likely to want to see AI in the metaverse as human-like robots or avatars.

MONEY

All commentators have acknowledged that the metaverse will feature its own internal economy, where participants will be able to earn, pay, exchange, and invest in currencies that exist entirely in the digital space, and not outside of it. Though it seems certain, as currently happens now, real world currency will be exchangeable with digital currencies that only exist in the metaverse.

What is a digital economy?

To make this clearer, we can imagine a coin that only appears in the metaverse. We'll call it a Metacoin. For convenience's sake, imagine it is a gold-looking coin, which is 3D. You can look at it through your VR headset and your avatar can hold it in their digitally created hand.

A friend can *give* you another Metacoin to add to your Metacoin. A different friend can give you another Metacoin.

You now have three Metacoin. Each of your friends has one fewer Metacoin than they had before.

Your avatar walks into digital shop that sells unique hair designs. You think your avatar will look good with that hair design, and are assured by the virtual shop assistant that this hair design does not exist anywhere else in the metaverse. It is completely unique. You pay the shop assistant with one of your Metacoin. The shop now has one more Metacoin than they had, but also one fewer unique hair designs. You have one fewer Metacoin, but your avatar is now wearing a lovely new hairstyle that *no-one else has.*

A stranger's avatar approaches you. They like your new hairstyle. They really like it. They like it so much they decide they want it. Because you are entrepreneurial, you say you will sell it to them, but for two Metacoin. The stranger agrees. You give them the hairstyle, they give you two Metacoin, and you part ways. You now have four Metacoin, but only your original avatar's hair.

This is all very basic, but this is an economy in action: there is the power to give currency from one owner to another; a creator can create something unique (the hairstyle); the creator may have had to pay someone else, perhaps a supplier or a digital platform, for the raw goods or foundation code to make the hairstyle; they are able to sell it to you; you are able to sell it to someone else, for more than you bought it for, so you make a profit.

In this simple case, no money comes into the metaverse from outside. No money leaves the metaverse. It is a closed economy where the same Metacoin move around and around the digital economy, in a blissful never ending circle.

Economies don't work that way, and the metaverse's internal economy will be far more complex, as we are about to see. But this easy exchange of goods will be its foundation.

How to make money from the metaverse

This is entirely different from making money *in* the metaverse, and needs to be treated separately. Though, like everything in the metaverse, there will be some overlap between the digital and the real.

As the metaverse continues to develop, it will offer lots of opportunities for the right people, in the right places, to make investments in the right funds, stocks, individual companies, and even single entrepreneurs.

That is because there's a lot of work to do. And there will be a lot of companies and individuals wanting a slice of pie.

If, for example, any meaningful experience of the metaverse is going to require some kind of VR headset then there will be companies that need to make that hardware on a large scale.

A survey by Immersion Promotion Design found that 4% of UK households own a VR headset. The US market cannot be dissimilar. For the metaverse to spread, production and development needs to massively increase. The consumer VR market worldwide was predicted to reach $3.7 billion at the end of 2021. Worldwide spending on AR/VR is likely to reach $72.8 billion by 2024. According to Statista, the number of VR/AR devices shipped worldwide is expected to increase to 68.6 million units in 2023. What's more, AR and VR headsets are projected to have massive sales of over 30 million units annually by the end of 2023.

Repeat those statistics for other necessary hardware and software for the metaverse: gloves and suits, sensors, screens, cables, mobile devices, consoles and much more, and the value of creating and sustaining the metaverse becomes enormous.

So, investment in the companies that design, manufacture, market, import and sell this hardware is likely to be something many are interested in.

Likewise, there will be opportunities to invest in already large companies that are involved in the future internet's development. From those that build and install cabling into our roads and houses, to those who design and lead with the software, ideas, surveying, monitoring, and evaluating.

Metaverse commentators also suggest that the metaverse will be far from a market for the big players only. Some believe some larger ones won't survive the transition, while smaller more innovative ones will find niches only they can fill. Smaller innovative companies, including individuals or small code programming teams, are very likely to contribute, and profit hugely.

"The 'creator economy' is about unleashing creativity - enabling anyone to earn a living or build a business around an audience, unconstrained by the high technological barriers that existed in the past," writes Jon Radoff on Medium.com.

An investment or a funding opportunity taken in one of those small companies that creates something unique, that is then rolled out into the metaverse, or the rights to use it are bought up by one of the bigger companies, could generate some serious money.

WhatsApp was founded and developed by Jan Koum and Brian Acton who previously worked at the search website Yahoo! They sold the App to Facebook in 2014 for $16 billion, including $12 billion in Facebook shares.

A serious investor could also look at the wider picture,

considering companies that provide services that make the metaverse tick. Everything from the manufacture of the cardboard boxes that VR headsets will be delivered in, to the supply and roll out of cable connections. From real estate to act as a work base for the promised 100,000 new staff Meta is intending to employ in mainland Europe; to drawing up and servicing complex new legal contracts to deal with the unique issues the metaverse is likely to breed. From merchandise to hardware, from retail to customer services and insurance. All will be opportunities, and none of them will involve entering the metaverse at all.

Cryptocurrency

Before we can look at the idea of earning money *within* the metaverse, it is important to understand what a digital currency is, and what can be done with it.

In old time gaming, a player would earn points, or coins, or rewards, or tokens for good performance in the game: completing a level, beating a bad guy, or solving a puzzle. They could then 'spend' these rewards on upgrades to their weaponry, avatar or buy bling for their car. In racing games, they might buy a better car, making them more likely to win the next race. A football manager might spend their winnings on better players.

These days, things are little more complex. At will, gamers can earn digital currency from their action in the game or platform, including just for turning up. But they can spend and swap that currency too, with far more choice than they had before. They can use that currency to build things and sell things. Vitally, they can spend real world money to buy virtual currency and spend that too. And in many platforms, they can take that money back out, including profits.

In Minecraft SandBox for example, players can spend real world money in the game, by simply going to an online shop. Outside of Minecraft, they can buy Minecoin on cards from gaming shops, or even a local newsagent. They put in the code, and the amount appears in their Minecoin account. They then use that Minecoin to buy in-game experiences, new skins, or to enter new Minecraft worlds created by others. Minecraft does not let you take money out of the game, so you can't exchange Minecoins back into real world dollars or pounds.

In the metaverse, this restriction is not likely to be the case. In fact, it is likely to be necessary for investors of all kinds to want to get involved in building, creation, entrepreneurialism and forging the new world from within the platform.

Simply put, if money earned by creators within the metaverse can only be spent further within the metaverse, then that currency will reach a peak of value for investors who will go and find a different way to make real money they can spend on their families, real food, real holidays, and other real stuff for their homes.

Non-fungible assets and tokens

These are likely to be terms you've heard in relation to the metaverse, but also outside of it. You may have no clear idea what they mean.

The term 'non-fungible assets' (NFAs) means items that hold value because of their unique makeup. Imagine a diamond, which has its own weight, cuts, and mass. There is no other diamond like it. It has a value, depending on how much someone is willing to pay for it. But it can't simply be swapped with another different diamond, with entirely different features.

In the same way, a piece of land is a non-fungible asset. It is in a specific place, with specific traffic passing, specific resources close by, specific weather, and specific makeup of soil. People will pay for the land, depending on *their* needs. But if you were to pick up the piece of land and put it somewhere else, well, it would be a different piece of land in a different place.

A 'non-fungible token' (NFT) is a certificate of ownership of a non-fungible asset that exists only in the digital world. This already exists, such as the online-only artwork work by Beeple, which was sold at Christies for $69.3 million. The artwork itself could not be given from one party to another, because it only exists in the digital world.

In order for the owner to prove ownership of this artwork, they needed a non-fungible token. This NFT cannot be copied or faked because it is contained within an isolated blockchain (see next section).

In the metaverse, where entrepreneurs will be creating and selling everything from computer code to unique avatar skins, from one-time hairstyles to individually created murals on your walls, these will be NFAs that only exist digitally. They will need to be represented too, by these certificates of ownership called NFTs that cannot be copied. When you buy a NFA from someone, you will exchange the NFT that represents the thing you are buying.

Don't worry if your head feels like it's going to explode. The metaverse will take care of the detail, you'll just own the goods.

Blockchains

These are perhaps the hardest to understand aspect of digital finance, though the term is thrown around quite carelessly as if most of us understand what a 'blockchain' is. They already exist and will be vital for the security of digital money in the metaverse. This is how they work.

Imagine a single list of people and the amount of x-coin they own. Tim has 100 x-coin. Bharat has 50 x-coin. Sam has 75 x-coin. Themba has 25 x-coin. That list is called a blockchain. At any time, Tim, Bharat, Sam and Themba have a full copy of that list. The list is also distributed in other places for security checking. The total value of that list (blockchain) of x-coin is 250 x-coin.

You cannot remove x-coin from the blockchain. You cannot put x-coin into the blockchain. You can only exchange within the blockchain. Tim gives Themba 25 x-coin. Tim now has 75 x-coin. Themba now has 50 x-coin. And the data is updated on everyone's list, as well as wherever the list has been stored on the internet.

No single person or entity owns the list. It just exists by virtue of being used. Say a bad guy wanted to steal some x-coin from Sam. They might be able to do that, but the x-coin would not disappear from Sam's account, because all the other copies of the list would show that Sam still owns those x-coin. They are just re-instated. In the meantime, the x-coin the bad guy has stolen are worthless outside of their list of x-coin.

The blockchain is secure exactly because it is not owned, but rather the data is shared among its users. It doesn't even need those users to trust each other. And in reality, the data about other users (our Bharat, Themba and Sam) wouldn't be known to Tim either.

This offers a few benefits to the metaverse.

First, value (money) can be exchanged within the metaverse securely. It will not be possible to steal that value.

Second, any user can - with the right platform - create their own blockchain, with its own online currency. This may be useful if, for example, George wants to create a project - like a building in the metaverse - and requires some real life investors to help fund the purchase of landscape in the metaverse, plus a digital architect, and 'digital raw materials'.

George can create a blockchain and currency of, say 1,000 George-coin. He can sell as many George-coin in the blockchain as he likes, as long as he doesn't go over the 1,000 George-coin that exists. His investors will then own George-coin as an investment in that specific project. If the building goes on to make a profit, say from virtual residents once it is built, the value of his George-coin in the real world will increase. It'll cost more real dollars to purchase one George-coin.

His investors could then sell George-coin back to George, or on an open virtual currency market, for their own profit. But of course, the project might fail, and they may not be able to sell their George-coin. And George is under no obligation to buy back that coin, unless that was a contracted element of his original sale.

Of course, blockchains, digital currencies and NFAs and NFTs are far more complex than I have attempted to outline. But I hope this offers an introduction to how finance will work in the metaverse.

In which case, how might someone make some of this money within the metaverse itself? The answer is as wide as your imagination.

How to make money *in* the metaverse?

Be an investor

Moving neatly from George and his George-coin, there will be opportunities within the metaverse for all of us, not just speculative investors, to put money into projects in the digital space. On a small scale, it wouldn't be surprising to see existing crowdfunding platforms like Go Fund Me, Kickstarter and Crowdcube getting in on the action.

That will mean you, as an individual, will be able to put small amounts of money into metaverse projects you've been convinced are worthwhile, or which you think might make you a profit. You won't have to find a fund manager or specific companies to invest in. This is a good example of a service platform in the metaverse that enables users to make the most of platforms that exist to achieve their goals.

For the bigger fish, it is likely that buyers will be able to directly purchase digital stock in metaverse projects such as land or building development, and earn returns when those projects are sold on, or rented. But they will also be able to invest in metaverse specific funds which spread the risk by investing smaller amounts across a number of virtual projects, as chosen by virtual fund managers, themselves earning their keep. This will operate exactly as it does in the real world, but could happen entirely in the metaverse.

Be a coder

The metaverse will be built out of at least three layers of coding. First, there will be open raw code that only those who know computer programming will touch. Second, there will be open platforms with existing coding 'blocks' that more amateur coders can build together to produce something new. Third, there will be ready-made platforms where any metaverse user might be able to build or design something, using the tools provided. Imagine an online garden planner, or an online T-shirt design program.

Each of these layers are likely to offer the opportunity to make money. The metaverse will require a constant pool of talented raw coders in order to make the metaverse happen, and for it to develop. Google's freelance coding staff already outnumber those who work directly for the company. For every new initiative those authoring projects in the metaverse pursue, they will need coders who sell their time and skill. In the same way, entrepreneurs with the great ideas, but not the technical skill, will hire freelances to make their dreams come to life - just as in the real world.

Note too, those freelance coders are likely to want to design their own codes, games, ideas as a side- or even main hustle, always knowing that if they strike just the right trend, or meet a particular need with their metaverse invention, it'll be snapped up for millions or even billions.

Be an entrepreneur

Likewise, those on the second and third level will be able to profit. They will be able to pay for existing platforms to provide them with code and tools to create their own products and ideas, without needing any detailed coding knowledge.

A clothes designer does not need to create their own design program within the metaverse in order to go about their business. They can pay to have access to an existing design program, that will allow them to use colors, techniques, patterns, presentation opportunities, and marketing plans to create unique clothes, that they can sell as non-fungible assets, thereby making money.

The owners of these platforms will earn money, and the designers themselves will also make money.

And on it goes. We can imagine any number of financial opportunities within the metaverse that offers opportunities to earn, from being a physical worker to a building firm constructing a big virtual building, to being the architect of that building. There's retail, inventions, education, training, sport, metaverse services, information, research. Any number of things can be monetized in the metaverse, and this is exactly what its architects hope for.

Be a celebrity

Whether you are a known name in the real world, with a personal presence in the virtual world, or only famous in the metaverse, you can make money in all the usual ways: sponsorship, gigs, turning up, recommending and reviewing, launching your own brand of virtual goods and more.

Gamers and YouTubers have made the most of this trend on the internet of today. People will sit for hours to watch YouTube videos for tips, a laugh or to look at cute cats. Bring in some sponsorship, or get paid by YouTube for the adverts that appear alongside your video, launch some merch alongside your videos, and you can make serious money.

To mention just a few YouTubers that appear across my kid's screens: Dude Perfect are worth $30 million, Mr Beast is worth $16 million, and Jeffree Star crushes the nearest competitor four times over with $200 million, according to Commoncentsmom.com. Though the last do now have a substantial side-line in cosmetics, due to their YouTube presence.

Be a gambler

Perhaps a less developed form of investing, it remains to be seen how far gambling will take its place in the metaverse. Certainly, gambling has found a place in the modern internet, offering betters the chance to make (and lose!) real money even on computer generated outcomes. But as the online space has opened up to gambling, governments have in turn been restricting and managing it better, urging and demanding gambling companies do what they can to limit overspends and addiction.

Later, we will tackle the issue of government and legal intervention in the metaverse, but it is worth stating now that when gambling companies do start to show real interest in the metaverse: everything from offering betting platforms to advertising off-line betting, there will arise the challenge of the health and welfare of those who participate.

One way or another, the metaverse is likely to be a ripe place to make and lose money by gambling, or by any other means. The contradictions that emerge from that are not inconsiderable, and will be a challenge into the future. For example, gambling is near-illegal in Cambodia, Qatar, United Arab Emirates, Singapore and North Korea, and in the United States in Utah and Hawaii.

Be a 'worker'

Like in the real world, the metaverse will create work opportunities that will exist only in the virtual or augmented reality world. In a creator-led economy, there will be a constant need for coders and others experienced in computer schematics and planning. But there will also be straight forward every day 'jobs' that need to be carried out in the metaverse that artificial intelligence (AI) can't do, or has not yet developed the ability to do.

Perhaps a company wants to commission an online-only artwork, to decorated its online building, or an online-only logo. Perhaps another company wants unique music composed for its leisure areas. Another wants a copywriter to write online-only advertising that works with a particular audience. All of these are skilled jobs that freelancers or small companies will be able to deliver, while the larger companies will be happy to outsource.

Other creators, such as flower arrangers, clothes designers, architects, tour guides, language teachers - the list is endless - will be able to offer their services entirely within the metaverse, delivering non-fungible assets and services in exchange for money.

But there may also be more 'menial' tasks to do in the metaverse that part-time or occasional workers will take on. They might create an opportunity for parents who have only occasional non-scheduled time to spare, students trying to supplement their income, and those who have grown up without a decent education or the opportunities that others have.

TikTok, for example, outsources its fact checking to an external company. These could just as well be freelancers logging on and seeing any number of facts, and are paid for each one they check.

Fiverr is already an online workplace where freelancers across the world can do various creative, design, coding, and other tasks for users, earning tiny amounts of money for each 'gig', but perhaps a decent amount for their country's average wage when all is considered. In the metaverse, these small jobs - the coding of a neon sign; creating a survey; analyzing some data - are likely to increase.

Axie is a Pokémon-like video game in which players can earn virtual currency from breeding and trading cute little pets called Axies on their mobile phones, or in internet cafes. To many players, it's just a harmless game. But to others, for example most of the 60% of players in the Philippines, it is replacing real jobs because players can earn more in the game, than in the real world.

In an extensive article, and later on a YouTube video, Leah Callon-Butler shows how Philippine kids and adults earn $300 to $400 dollars a week (a lot in the Philippines). They exchange the tokens they've won in Axie for cryptocurrencies, then again into real money.

To players who would otherwise be living in poverty, she writes, "play-to-earn looks pretty good. So good, in fact, that I've heard a few murmurs that we might soon see increasing numbers of workers ditching their offline jobs to seek a career in the Metaverse instead."[1]

In a YouTube video, Jeffrey Jiho Zirlin, co-founder of Axie, says: "With the pandemic, it's destroyed a lot of physical jobs. In many cases, permanently. So I think what we're dealing with is a fundamental change in the nature of work."

In fact, new 'Axie universities' are emerging, where collectives are buying 'Axies' and renting them out to players, so even without having to pay for increasing costs to enter the game, players can earn a little to start with, then enter the market for themselves proper. This may well be what a metaverse economy begins to look like.

While Axie seems happy to support this type of earning, there exists a grey economy of 'gold mining', where players (mostly in the lower income world) spend all day in a game, collect trophies, coins, and other things of virtual value, and then sell them to people in the higher income world for real money.

Their aim isn't to accumulate points or win, it is to go around collecting bling to sell. Though most games attempt to ban this, it is easy to see how something similar might become lucrative in the metaverse for those with limited skill, but lots of time to exploit.

Be at the cross over

Perhaps one of the early opportunities in the metaverse is already well underway, where physical brands and retail are exploring their opportunities to market and sell non-fungible assets in the online world.

Already, Nike has filed trademarks for selling digital clothes, shoes, and other branded items with its famous swoosh logo to be worn in online only worlds. Users will be able to pay for unique specially designed sneakers, that no-one else owns, and wear them in the metaverse.

According to the British Daily Mail, Gucci is already selling a pair of shoes for £8.99 that could only be worn virtually. A digital rendition of the Gucci Dionysus bag sold for 350,000 Robux (roughly $4,115) on Roblox, more than the real life version of the bag costs.

Fashion brand ASOS has had an augmented reality presence since 2019, with a feature called the Virtual Catwalk. It allows users to see ASOS designs on virtual bodies like their own.

The tool shows shoppers how products realistically look in different sizes, and on different body types. The initiative helps to drive sales as well as reduce returns in the real world.

Opportunities are abound for retailers and consultants who already exist in the real world, to build their offer in the metaverse. Retailers as small as a single coffee shop could create a virtual version of their own premises, so potential customers can get an impression of their offering, their ambiance, and clientele. Hopefully, they will persuade customers to visit them in real life.

In the meantime, consultants in everything from finance to advertising, will be able to build businesses advising companies on how to make the most of the metaverse, by being the bridge between them and the virtual world.

A key challenge

As with any financial development, there are likely to be some financial growing pains experienced by the metaverse and its major and minor players. For all involved, especially in the early stages, it is likely to be about co-operation and interaction between platforms.

We still live in a world where anything designed for Mac won't run on PCs, and vice versa. Apps, while are still split between Android and iOS platforms on cell phones, are brutally incompatible. I can't send an iPhone picture message to an Android phone, without it being converted to a (costly) text message. FaceTime is readily available on iPhones, but only available for Android users via a browser extension. Speaking of browsers, Macs run Safari, Windows runs Microsoft Edge and Google runs Chrome. None of them are designed to work nicely with each other. It has only been since 2020 that Amazon's Kindles would accept non-Kindle eBook files.

One can imagine the race is on for many of the larger companies to create a user friendly currency for the metaverse, and the financial tools to effectively manage it, before a competitor. They want *their* currency to become the *de facto* online financial system.

Smaller players like the already popular Bitcoin may stand a chance achieving this domination. But something backed by a big name like Meta (Facebook), Amazon, Windows, or Google is likely to bring with it more credibility and trust by sheer brand power. Later, I discuss how larger companies will *have* to work together if the kind of metaverse that is imagined is to come about.

This race for domination of a currency may be the acid test of how willing they are to work together to create a Metacoin, rather than separate, albeit interchangeable currencies, for each platform.

Take aways

- The metaverse will have its own digital economies, with currencies exchangeable within platforms, and between the metaverse and the real world.
- The generation of the metaverse will create huge investment, invention and employment opportunities.
- Cryptocurrency will be central to the metaverse, with creators, gamers and investors, earning money within the metaverse itself.

- Individuals will be able to own goods in the metaverse, with non-fungible tokens signifying their ownership, protected by blockchains.
- There is a race to become the *de facto* currency in the metaverse, with all major players already generating their own.

WORK

Before 2020, there was a general trend in the higher income world for more people who could work from home, to do so - at least for some part of the week. Many companies, such as the UK communication giant BT, invested millions on setting up employees with their own home office, equipment, and high speed broadband. Moving out of expensive office buildings saved them far more than it cost to do that. Employees at certain locations would still come in to 'hot desk' at central offices and for some meetings, but the idea of their own desk and their own office at a building didn't make financial sense.

"Our first home working trials were back in 1992," writes Dr Nicola J. Millard, Principal Innovation Partner at BT. "By 2000, a significant part of our workforce worked from home. I spent much of the 1990s interviewing BT homeworkers and making sure they had everything they needed to work effectively."

In Millard's effective home working advice to employees, she encourages them to use video conferencing frequently, make space for 'water cooler moments', 'keep the conversation going with chat and social media', but warns not all colleagues will want to use video chat, particularly if they're having a 'bad hair day'.

She concludes: "We're in the midst of a big global shift in remote, virtualized digital working. Our experiences in BT have shown that, done well, home working can be an extremely fulfilling and productive way of working. But it may take a while for all of us to establish new habits and routines. The results of this experiment will be fascinating, but one thing's for sure: the ways we work are likely to change forever."

The impact of Covid-19

It wasn't long before companies were forced to adopt the BT model, though many were already well on board. Across the world, Covid-19 struck at the end of 2019, and governments introduced various forms of 'lock down'.

In the UK, it became illegal for a time for people to leave their own homes for anything except up to an hour of exercise. Some companies were forced to close entirely, and governments introduced compensation schemes. But others were relatively quickly able to adapt, by introducing and stepping up the kind of home working for which pioneers had paved the way.

Zoom had ten million daily meeting participants in December 2019, but by April 2020, that number had risen to over 300 million.

In a Covid-19 world, it seems clear that the workplace may never look the same again. Apart from a small proportion of detractors, and of course those who cannot carry out their business online, like manufacturers and hospitality locations, business and the workplace in monolithic multi-floor multi-occupancy buildings is slowly being replaced by far more working from home.

Covid-19 has been proof positive for companies that home working (or 'distributed teams' as it is often called) can improve production and save them money.

The appearance of the metaverse, and its multiple tools to improve workplace productivity, virtual meeting space, virtual reality, improved social media communications, and perhaps most importantly the ability to jointly create and design in a single virtual space, does not come as a coincidence with Covid-19.

It is clear that Covid-19 was a factor in the increased desire for this kind of working environment. It was the trigger that made companies look differently at the future workplace. Perhaps without the global pandemic, our rush to the metaverse would have been far slower.

Speaking to Forbes.com, Kate Lister, president of Global Workplace Analytics, said: "Seventy-seven percent of the workforce say they want to continue to work from home, at least weekly, when the pandemic is over." Lister estimates, "Twenty-five to 30% of the workforce will be working-from-home multiple days a week by the end of 2021."

Research quoted by Harvard Business Review found the same attitude to home working.

Knowledge workers "spent 12% less time drawn into large meetings and 9% more time interacting with customers and external partners. Lockdown also helped people take responsibility for our own schedules. They did 50% more activities through personal choice and half as many because someone else asked them to. Finally, during lockdown, people viewed their work as more worthwhile. The number of tasks rated as tiresome dropped from 27% to 12%, and the number we could readily offload to others dropped from 41% to 27%."[1]

Most of the companies that have already said they are committed to 'distributed teams' working forever do, of course, include most of the big players in the internet space: Google, Amazon, Facebook (now Meta), Apple, Reddit, Quora, HubSpot, DropBox, Twitter and more. But they also include finance, insurance, and management: Lincoln Financial Group, Nationwide Insurance, Siemens, Square, and Verizon.

So, given much of it will be working from home, or remote working, what can we expect from the metaverse in terms of our newly styled workplaces?

The metaverse workplace

Remote team meetings

In the workplace, the ability to meet with others for open discussion is regarded as vital. But in the past, has also been the bane of people's working lives: unnecessary meetings, meetings about meetings, meetings that run over, unannounced unplanned meetings, and meetings you didn't realize were meetings.

With the growth of online meetings, via Zoom, Google Hangouts or Microsoft Teams, its proponents argue that meetings are generally more focussed, time limited, and productive. Meetings for socializing, 'water cooler moments' as BT would have it, are arranged specifically for that purpose, allowing for a business, finance, or strategic meeting to be just that.

As Microsoft claims for its Teams product: "Meet in a

more engaging and meaningful way with a video conference call and empower teamwork and productivity in the moment."

A report by Forbes.com, published in early 2020 argues there "are five key reasons why video conferencing is superior to audioconferencing, and can often be even more effective than face-to-face meetings". It includes improved engagement, efficiency, better communication, and learning, helps dispersed teams keep connected, and helps to get things done.

If we accept this effort to bring us all online for meetings, then the metaverse is certainly likely to be the space where that will take place.

In his launch of Meta on November 28, 2021, Mark Zuckerberg takes viewers on a virtual tour of the metaverse as his company sees it. It should be noted, many of the ideas and tools he shows don't actually exist yet. But they present a vision of what Meta is looking forward to.

In the work section of the video, he presents a vision of an architect working from home. The man brings up a holographic version of a building he's working on, and then calls for a colleague (who's relaxing in the park) into a 'real quick get together for a debrief'.

She comes into his home, in holographic form too, and they both go inside the building before he declares 'I think it's ready'.

Note, this isn't virtual reality. They're not looking at each other's 3D avatars. They are looking at each other's real bodies, albeit in holographic form. They can see each other, hear each other, and enter a virtual hologram of the building they've designed together.

Later, the holographic version of the architect joins a meeting in the 3D virtual world. There, his colleagues are in avatar form, as well as on video screens. What Meta are showing here is that the barrier between real life, video conferencing, holographic presentation, and virtual avatars won't be an either/or option. They will be integrated.

It's clear even from the video that Meta is far away yet. Zuckerberg tells its audience they are currently working on a virtual meeting room that users will be able to brand for themselves, and put up posters! (My exclamation. You would be thinking he'd be reaching for something more challenging).

That seems a lot different from virtually entering a 3D holographic building, but the prediction is probably a good one.

The metaverse will allow us to engage in multi-media virtual meetings of all kinds, and a mix of kinds, depending on what software, hardware, and equipment we have. It won't depend on one single platform or tool, but may unite various methods to make virtual meetings a workable proposition.

As Zuckerberg concludes: "Giving people the tools to be present wherever they are, whether they are a hologram sitting next to you in a physical meeting, or in a discussion taking place in the metaverse, it's going to be a game changer."

The Meta platform where this revolution takes place will be its Horizon Workrooms. The British technology company Virtulab have developed an "immersive virtual venue" that can be hired. Though currently you visit it on a 2D screen, the impression you get is of 3D bodies walking around a 3D world, including realistic looking bot-people who can help you navigate. It has been used by TEDx and the Institute of People Management. It's not difficult to see how this platform might quickly go immersive when the technology exists.

As well as Zoom and Microsoft teams, there are other serious players in this space, offering remote workers more than just a gallery of faces on a screen.

Wonder provides a simple webpage full of bubbles, each containing a photo of a guest, moving between white circles meant to represent tables on which people can video chat with each other. Its users include Deloitte and Harvard.

The platform Gather offers a fun interaction, in user picked blocky avatars in specific rooms, and enables its four million users to interact including through speech, video and sharing information and images.

All of which begs the question: why go further? If some of the platforms that currently exist are already doing a good job of allowing us to interact with work colleagues visually and audibly at the touch of a button. And we can share and edit documents in real time, meet as a group and individually, and use all of these together throughout our working day to get the job done, why do we need a virtual experience of the same thing?

Why do we need to do this in a virtual world, when we can already look at a 2D screen, and speak into a microphone, and get pretty much the same experience?

Mark Zuckerberg argues in TheVerge, "a lot of that time we're spending, we're basically mediating our lives and our communication through these small, glowing rectangles. I think that that's not really how people are made to interact."

He complains about grids of faces, no sense of space, no sense of where sounds and voices are coming from, and sometimes finding it "hard to remember what meeting someone said something in because they all look the same and they all blend together."

He concludes: “What virtual and augmented reality can do, and what the metaverse broadly is going to help people experience, is a sense of presence that I think is just more natural in the way that we’re made to interact.”

Some might argue this is rich coming from the founder of a company that developed Facebook and owns WhatsApp, both platforms that perhaps more than others have zapped our natural instinct to ‘experience a sense of presence’ with other people.

Zoom fatigue

But another challenge is the emergent trend, already recognized in 2020, and more substantially in 2021, of ‘Zoom fatigue’.

In the journal Technology, Mind and Behavior, Professor Jeremy Bailenson, founding director of the Stanford Virtual Human Interaction Lab, has assessed Zoom, and by implication all video-conferencing applications, and has identified four consequences of prolonged video chats that he says contribute to the syndrome.

High levels of eye-to-eye contact is highly intense; seeing yourself constantly in video-chats is stressful; video chats dramatically reduce our real mobility; in virtual chats we have to work harder to send and receive signals, because our ability to gesture, move our faces, and show emotion is reduced. We also get highly distracted by the things in people’s backgrounds, meaning we have to work harder mentally to pay attention.

Arguably, each of these challenges are likely to be of issue also in a three dimensional world. Staring at a screen is simply hard work and our eyes will get tired. The idea of enjoying a meeting with colleagues while wearing a VR headset on the treadmill or a static cycle is a stereotype. The rest of us will be sitting at a desk, not moving around. We may be seeing ourselves, once again, worrying about whether the avatar we've chosen is appropriate, looks good, or is being judged. And our gestures in the metaverse will not be smooth or humanlike. Not least, because in order to get very specific, millimeter by millimeter tracking of our bodies, we're going to have to wear suits and set up cameras that can see our every move.

But there's more. I can't watch my son play FIFA 21 on his PlaysStation without feeling sick. It's the jerky movements of players running forwards and backwards, up and down. That doesn't mirror watching a real football game at all because my head is still. I am not moving my body as I might watching a real football match, or even one on TV.

Zuckerberg has already admitted that VR headsets are heavy and cumbersome, and stated his intention to develop thinner glasses that can give us a full augmented, if not virtual reality, experience. Apple has been promising the same for over ten years.

Health and welfare

If you've ever worn a VR headset, and used it to explore an adventure, or look around, you may have found it quite heavy to wear. If you have used it to drive a virtual car, ride a rollercoaster, or do anything quick moving, you may also have been made to feel quite queasy. Where companies and individuals might benefit from working via VR headsets, and statically from their own desks, a solution will need to be found in the real world for possible increase in fatigue, back problems, neck issues (due to heavy headsets), decreased mobility, poor mental health, and loneliness.

Wired magazine reported a 2020 survey by employment law firm Slater and Gordon which found that 34% of British women, attending online visual meetings like on Zoom, were asked to wear more makeup or change their hair, while 27% were told to "dress more sexy or provocatively."

"If the internet has amplified societal flaws, the metaverse risks supercharging them," the writer concludes.

Video conferencing is not a panacea. It will still allow people to be drawn into last minute, stressful and lengthy meetings, when they could be more effectively working. While it might reduce workplace bullying and prejudice - many virtual meetings will be recorded - at the same time, the lack of face-to-face contact and real emotion shared might prevent someone from picking up on a colleague's real distress, mental health state or loneliness.

And as Slater and Gordon found, it might lead to people feeling the need to constantly be on show, updating and perfecting themselves and their avatars to display new expectations of what your avatar *should* look like at work. And this may add to stress.

In Microsoft's Horizon, avatars don't have legs, their mouths don't move, their eyes don't make contact with each other. An experience which Peter Rubin from Wired states is "not, not creepy". They are far away from the interactive emotional experience that metaverse advocates envisages.

If we're asked to engage constantly online, mostly with VR and AR headsets to chat with our colleagues in virtual space, there will be an awful long way to go before the experience is genuinely enjoyable and practical. And users will need to be convinced of the benefits, compared with simply video calling, emailing, messaging, or even picking up the phone while still wearing your pajamas.

Equality of opportunity in the workplace

Not every worker will have decent internet speeds, nor will they be able to afford the necessary kit to work in the metaverse for long periods of time.

While larger companies may find value in correcting this, if they are to be in the metaverse they will have to 'kit out' everyone from those in the top levels of management, to those in the post room on minimum wages.

Companies may not find it financially viable to do this for the lower echelons of their company, instead gathering that class of workers together in cheap physical workplaces, on the edge of towns. This may create extreme inequality, and could breed animosity.

Even for the upper echelons, it will benefit most those who live in urban areas, where internet connections are fast and stable. Those managers and white collar workers who have chosen to leave the rat race and live in suburban or even country properties might not get the super-fast broadband they and their companies need. There may be a cost-benefit analysis for companies to make about whether to pay for them to be 'plugged in' properly, or to insist they come into work.

And that's just the big companies.

Smaller, companies - in the UK they are defined as having £6.5 million turnover ($8.7 million) and not having more than 50 employees - are less likely to invest in fast internet connections for each of their employees, let alone VR kit. Because of rapid turnover of staff and flexibility, arming everyone with metaverse equipment may be too costly. Smaller companies might reject it altogether and continue to plod along. Despite the 'opportunity' the big players are offering, smaller companies might find it more viable to invest in their product or service than in inter-company virtual meetings. After all, Zoom or the phone is already available.

Employees off grid

People's individual right to privacy, to not share their data, and to exclude themselves from the metaverse is an issue of its own (tackled later). But in the workplace, it will be worth noting here.

Currently, it is illegal for a worker or prospective employee to be discriminated on the base of sexual orientation, class, background, race, religion, political persuasion, trade union membership and any other number of cases (with sound exceptions to the rules too). And rightly so.

But this does raise the issue of whether someone who has freely chosen not to become part of the new internet world, or at least not to share all of their data on a daily basis, might not be able to get the career or opportunities they want. And indeed, the same for those who cannot afford to be fully connected up.

Will employers be able to demand, ahead of recruiting someone, that workers have a fast internet connection, an Oculus headset (so they're compatible with the rest of the company), and a private office so that kids or pets don't disturb work?

It's easy to say an employer should pay for this in someone's home working situation, but that's not realistic for small companies of, say, five to ten people. They may be forced to discriminate, because they can't afford to pay for teching up prospective employees.

The metaverse advocate's dream of an ever more creative, small contributor to a bigger picture narrative, seems less realistic when these factors are taken into account. Will we end up only with larger companies participating in the metaverse, creating a two-tier economy?

Not every job is online

Or maybe even a three-tier one? Because like it or not, not every operation can be carried out online, nor in a virtual space. In Covid-19, doctors have been able to reduce their face-to-face contact with patients, but there are times when your doctor needs to see you - and treat you - face-to-face.

You can send them all the pictures you have of that lump in your breast, but she is going to want to feel, press and take a sample of it at some point. And the sooner the better.

In everything from retail to food supply, medicine to entertainment, construction and manufacturing, to shipping, waste management, and haircuts (as we all saw through our long fringes in the Covid-19 pandemic), there are many, many job roles that simply cannot be taken online.

Some because physically it's impossible. However much we live in the metaverse, and a virtual and augmented reality world, we're still going to need to live in houses, go to the toilet, eat, travel, wear clothes, and (possibly) go on holidays. All of these, and so many more, demand real people doing real jobs. They can't be carried out online, and certainly not by artificial intelligence (AI).

Other jobs won't go online because people's desire for real experiences are very likely to continue. For all the growth of eBooks and audio books, people still love and want the feel of a paperback or hardback in their hands, and on their shelves. People still want to browse garden centers, go to markets, meet for coffee, visit museums and leisure parks, go to the theatre and even to the cinema, to watch a film on a huge screen, with surround sound.

The metaverse will provide opportunities to do these things within its own platforms, and those experiences will be enjoyable in themselves. But no-one can claim they will be the same, or will adequately replace those physical experiences we all still enjoy.

And to deliver those still enjoyable experiences, there will need to be staffing. Workers. And lots of them. And very few will need to have any contact with the metaverse to do their jobs, even if the processing of their wages, their recruitment, their performance reviews, and decisions about who or what type of workers required takes place in virtual meetings between those who do use the metaverse.

Take aways

- Covid-19 created an unprecedented, but useful, opportunity for platforms to develop working from home, something the metaverse will take further.
- The metaverse will make it easy for remote team meetings, either in virtual reality or in a mix that doesn't require lots of individual boxes with faces in them.
- Improvements will be needed in virtual technology for meetings to feel comfortable,

such as better, lighter headsets, and prevention of Zoom fatigue.

- VR presents challenges to employers in terms of equality of opportunity and choice.
- Not every job is online, and many functions such as personal care require physical touch rather than virtual interaction.

EDUCATION

For all the gaming and work related benefits, it's easy to see how the world of education is likely to gain hugely from the metaverse. And to be more readily adopted by the generations of learners to follow.

It is safe to assume those in their younger educational years - from even kindergarten to university majors and beyond - are more comfortable with computers and technological advances, because they've been part of the generation that has grown up with it.

While my own middle age generation is mumbling to each other, 'it's amazing what they can do with computers these days', and my parents are staring at screens saying: 'how does this work again?' and calling on my kids to help them load an App, those below 25 are not just comfortable with high tech, they can't imagine life without it.

Introducing the benefits of the metaverse into the education they currently experience, at least in richer countries, is unlikely to feel very different from what they're already used to. In my own secondary school (aged 11-15) we had a 'computer room', full of bulky desk top computers, connected by thick cables, that had no connection to the outside world. It was a place for nerdy kids (including me) to go and try to write code in BASIC, the most simple coding language, because we were too shy to hang around the playground, due to not being able to play football.

My son, now pushing 12, has his own Chrome book which he brings home from school. My eldest, 13, has an iPad. Both have mobile phones and Kindle Fires. My eldest has a MacBook, my son has a PlayStation 4. It's embarrassing when you add it all up, but it's certainly not unusual - and we can (weakly) justify each piece of equipment.

My kids do their homework on their school issued computers. They submit homework on them. They carry out research. They look at each other's work. And during various Covid-19 lockdowns, Apps like Zoom and Google Classrooms were the only way they were able to stay in touch with their teachers and classes. Schools adapted to Covid-19, but it wasn't too difficult, because kids were already so used to sending emails, messaging their friends, playing multi-layer games, designing and drawing online, and reading and posting online.

When my kids are set homework - including my five year old - they're asked to research the subject on the internet. Mostly, that means watching YouTube videos, which is just fine for picking up headline ideas and facts.

Most schools and universities in the higher income world are not just ready for the metaverse, they're actively encouraging it, already using it on an almost daily basis to add depth to learning.

The question, like so many others in the internet of tomorrow, will be how these technologies are integrated into the metaverse, in the virtual world, and who will own them.

Virtual reality

In some sense, Meta (Facebook) was late to the party in the October 2021 launch video for the new company brand: a student is getting help on her astrophysics homework by swiping her hands to manipulate a giant picture of the solar system, zooming in on the rings of Saturn by gesturing with her arms.

"If you were taking astrophysics, you could study in the multiverse," said the narrator, Marne Levine, Meta's chief business officer.

The next example is a student wandering around ancient Rome, thanks to an immersive VR world where the student is transported as an avatar.

"Imagine standing on the streets hearing the sounds, visiting the markets," said Levine in the video's narration. "To get a sense of the rhythm of life more than 2,000 years ago. Imagine learning how the forum was built by actually watching the forum get built right in front of you."

Well, we don't need to imagine these things. They already exist, and have done for many years. In schools, in universities and in education research, teachers have been using virtual technology to bring learning to life, and to model and illustrate their own research.

There are already a number of companies who are creating educational virtual experiences, based on school and college curriculums.

Take the company Class VR for example. It supplies schools with value for money VR and AR headsets, and the virtual learning modules it has designed all follow the United States school curriculum.

The platform boasts 1,000 VR and AR modules, which allow teachers to give their pupils - of all ages - a virtual learning experience. Through the headsets, pupils can get up close and personal with everything from beating hearts, Second World War airplanes in flight, take a 3D look inside cells, go on a 'moon field trip', explore caves, visit historical buildings, and dive down to coral reefs.

Maths and English are just as well served, with virtual experiences on poetry, language, creative writing, and communication, and visualizations of 3D shapes, lines and measurement, parallel and perpendicular lines, and angles, estimation, and prediction.

Currently, these experiences are delivered in class, with pupils wearing the headsets in groups. But it's not difficult to imagine pupils in their individual homes doing the same, popping in and out of pre-programmed virtual experiences, to enter their virtual classroom to socialize with the avatars of their friends, and to work with their teacher's avatar.

The modules don't replace teacher-led learning, but the worksheets and the immersive experiences add to the class work, keeping it interesting and engaging.

But some have gone further than supplementing everyday school curriculums with AR and VR learning. Entrepreneurs in Florida have launched the American High School, a fully online and accredited educational institution, available to pupils the world over.

Steve Grubbs, CEO of VictoryXR, which is part of the pilot project said: "What American High School is launching are classes where students and their teacher will gather together in the same VR classroom space and interact as if they were in a physical school building."

Students will be able to handle human organs in biology class, construct molecules in chemistry class, and take field trips together for history class, all while learning in immersive ways with 3D objects and interactive environments.

"America's best hope is that students in our High School – even though they are in different time zones – can experience the power of learning communally. And if the data is correct about significantly improved retention, then American High School students will have a better learning experience in a more social environment, and that's a win-win for everyone," said Franz Schmelkes, Director of Strategy and Business at Qualcomm.

Younger kids love touching, pushing buttons, getting reactions, and doing experiments. The museums and galleries arena long ago realised this, and began to change stuffy 'do not touch' museums into fully interactive, physical learning experiences. Stroke the manta ray. Wind the pulley to lift the weight. Ride the bike to create electricity. See what happens when you place rocks in this flow of water. Shine this light through these different vessels of colored water.

Setting aside the excitement for kids of getting 'out of school' to go on field trips like these, along with the coach ride, the lunch boxes and exploding yoghurts, which are all part of the fun, it is easy to envisage a metaverse where most of these experiences can be reproduced. If easy-to-use responsive gloves can be created, for example, pupils may be able touch a virtual manta ray, watch it react, and to feel the roughness of its skin. They may be able to shine a virtual torch, and see the results in the colored water.

The experiences will not be exactly the same. Until we have chips installed in our brains, we will always know we're having a virtual reality experience, but as the metaverse develops it will become pretty close.

For younger pupils, VR and AR may provide great opportunities for them to interact with their learning. They will be able to 'touch' and see close up things they are learning about: the water cycle, bouncing numbers and letters, history, getting to know themselves, their culture and moderating behavior.

But there remains that question of unscheduled fun, sharing with friends with abandon, and enjoying the unpredictability of that yoghurt. Do we not learn, after all, not only from sterile, predictable experiences that cannot go wrong, but also from real life when Jimmy slips on the steps, Amina pees in her underwear, and Sam can't find their way out of the dinosaur gallery in time to catch the bus?

Artificial intelligence (AI) in education

It is likely that AI will also play a role in children's education. One can imagine even younger kids learning a language by speaking out loud to an AI French teacher, who responds directly and exactly to praise, correct, and move the conversation on.

AI could also set tests, automatically look for correct and incorrect answers, and offer scores and even extra points for effort, or for improvement based on a single pupil's past achievements, rather than just ranking them in a class.

But can AI look after the emotional, sensory, and pastoral needs of younger (and teen) pupils in schools. We all suspect that teachers working with this age group can be very flexible with the praise they offer kids, and any awards, merits, and certificates they give out. That's not judgement or preference, it's sound educational practice. If Helen isn't communicating well, but is particularly vocal on a given day, a teacher might reward that. While the most vocal in class doesn't get rewarded for speaking more.

Ronald is having difficulties at home, and not getting his homework done. An experienced and trained teacher can pick this up in class, and make space and accommodate that child's needs. It remains to be seen whether AI could get even close to that.

Which brings education in the metaverse to a key challenge. That of safeguarding children from harm, and supporting families that need it.

In the United Kingdom, schools offer early breakfast clubs and offer after school clubs for kids aged 4 to ten. The youngest kids across England get free meals at school. Across Europe there are similar initiatives. In the United States, pre-Covid-19, some 20.1 million kids got free lunches at school, and another nearly two million got lunches at just 40 cents.

The reason for this is that some families live in poverty, in chaos, and the children are vulnerable. In some households, children simply don't get to eat. Schools can be the only break children have from difficult situations at home. School is safe, they get fed, and teachers and pastoral staff can do what they can to relieve some of the difficulties they face.

Introducing the metaverse widespread into education and celebrating it because it frees up parents from bringing their kids to school, reduces school hours for kids and helps them to focus and explore more virtually, and to work in new and exciting ways, misses perhaps the social function of schools and the welfare of younger children and teens.

First, if visits to school become a rarity rather than the norm, teachers and pastoral class will have less contact with the pupils under their charge, and will not be able to pick up the subtle signs of underfeeding, neglect and even abuse.

Second, widespread movement to online teaching prevents the social experiences that kids need, that may not be accurately or effectively reproduced in the online world. Loneliness is real for five year olds, made only worse if they can't find any friends from class on their headsets.

Thirdly, a number of children may be excluded from schools and education if the metaverse develops without due note that some families cannot afford the equipment, or if given it by schools, may not see it as a priority for their children to use it.

In very chaotic families, where parents don't have the ability to ensure their children are fed and clothed, can it be expected that their kids will be plugged into their headsets on time, dressed, and ready to work each day?

Meta is investing millions in making education the center of its new mission and image. Roblox is spending $10 million to develop three different educational video platforms, aimed at younger, teenage, and university students, to help with learning. Each of the games will have its own focus: robotics, space exploration and, for the college-age users, careers, and fields like computer science, engineering, and biomedical science.

For all the investment going into the development of education through the metaverse, there might be questions about whether some of that money should also be spent ensuring children are safe, well fed, and able to access the same metaverse opportunities of their peers.

UNESCO, the United Nations body for education, argued in 2018 that good teaching is necessary to help children integrate new technologies into their learning.

Private companies should not be allowed to do it at all, because it needs to be built on the way children learn:

"Only comprehensive training on the integration of mobile technologies and appropriate pedagogical methodologies, as well as necessary subject matter knowledge, can equip teachers with adequate initial skills to design and facilitate mobile learning practices. Effective mobile learning projects also require ongoing support to guide teachers to use learner centered techniques."[1]

Universities

It is perhaps easier to see the roll out of the metaverse among older pupils, university and college students, those at vocational institutions, and among academia.

For older and university pupils, they will use the metaverse not only for virtual experiences, but they will also use the tools the new internet provides to learn more comprehensively, to research, to discuss new ideas, to design, to create, to share, and deliver.

Like it or not, Google has become a huge source of easy-to-access information for students and teachers, as well as authors writing about the metaverse. Other tools like Wikipedia, YouTube, virtual libraries, online catalogues of research papers, and free-to-download classic texts from Amazon and elsewhere, mean students can do more and more without leaving their laptops to go to the library.

When set an essay in theology at university, my first stop was to a clunky computer to find the location of the books I needed. The books existed somewhere in the enormous physical library in various places around the city. These books were on my 'reading list' and I was supposed to read all of them, before even starting my essay.

I'd then track those books down, and of course do what most of my peers were doing: go directly to the index page, look up the key words and references I thought I might need, then go directly into the book to the relevant chapters and read only those. Sometimes, only the pages I needed. I might be able to photocopy some of those most relevant pages (the books couldn't be taken out of the library) and use a highlighter pen to mark out the most relevant quotes and passages.

I'd then take the copies home, and gradually build up my essay. I was lucky enough to have my own desktop computer, so was able to write my essays on Microsoft Word. Others hand wrote their work.

Skip forward 30 years, and research looks very different indeed. For an essay on Greek philosophers, for example, I can download for free the actual texts, or read them online. I used to have to use a thick and heavy Bible concordance, to look at how Luke's gospel picks up references from the Old Testament. Now, I can go to Bibleonline.com and simply put in a search term, and quickly tell you there are exactly 617 references to 'water' in the whole Bible, and I can go directly to them.

I can now write my essay, or if more convenient speak it, and have it delivered to my tutor. We may enter a Zoom call to discuss it, or using some of the tools used by universities mentioned below, meet as virtual avatars. There's no reason why we couldn't create Roblox or Fortnite avatars for ourselves and meet there. We could look at my essay together in real time, and I could slide in suggestions as we speak. My tutor could add references, cut and paste passages from scholars, and suggest further reading which they swipe to my avatar in real time.

This all feels so much more convenient, and might

encourage even more in-depth exploration of the subject matter.

In the metaverse, there will be no more waiting for fellow students to finish with the books I need. There will be far quicker and direct access to the information I want. And it will be easier to do the work and deliver it to my tutors.

In some disciplines, theology perhaps included, there's no reason to suggest that AI couldn't do some of the work guiding students in the right direction, or analyzing our essays, mathematics, or even creative work.

But there's more to the university and the metaverse. The word university emerges from the Latin meaning 'the whole', the same routes as universal. It posits a situation not only of learning but of sharing.

Online lectures and conferences are nothing new in the age of YouTube and Covid-19, but the metaverse is likely to offer more flexible ways to engage with learning. While Zoom, Microsoft Teams and Google Classroom offer screens full of images of those engaged in a particular lecture, too many faces can be distracting, only one person can speak at a time, and naturally conversation tends to take place in a sidebar by text.

The metaverse might offer a different way of attending such events. Our avatars can visit a virtual lecture theatre. Before the lecture begins, we could freely engage with any of the other pupils attending. Though that lecture might be attended by hundreds, or even thousands of pupils, we might choose only to be able to see those in our college, or even in our class. We can chat directly to friends and fellow learners, with our voices and our avatars, zoning out the noise from other chats in real time (just as we do in real life) until the lecture begins.

Called to order, we will be able to attend the lecture, but go through it or any slides at our own pace. We'll mark what we are seeing for later follow up, and post real voice questions, or avatar quick videos for the lecturer to deal with later.

If asked by our tutor, we can gather into groups of any number of learners, to drill down our learning, and then return to the larger group with our responses. All written on a virtual white board, or even in a virtual 3D mind map structure.

We will be able to do research online during the lecture, or during group time then bring that research back, including 3D models that students can gather around, with lists of references for further studies.

And we will be able to get hands on with the subject our lecturer is talking about. In a medicine lecture, perhaps, our professor might spend half an hour outlining the cell makeup of a human liver. Afterwards, alone or in groups, pupils may be given their own virtual liver to 'dissect', take virtual photos of, and present back to our tutor. And our tutor will have a 3D video of all the processes we went through to get to that stage.

It's not difficult to see how these concepts could be rolled out across all subjects, from history to technology, mechanics to architecture, medicine to mathematical modeling.

Like never before, academics will be able to illustrate incredibly complex ideas. The mind naturally goes to the 3D representations many of us might have seen of the DNA coil, or more recently the spherical shape, surrounded by protruding crowns that illustrates the coronavirus. But these are only the start.

Like in the Meta video, students will be able to select a

planet from the solar system. Zoom in on it, using their hands in a pulling motion. Expand it, dig deeper into the surface of the planet, to discover its geological make up. From there, they might pull up information about a particular mineral, and head down that route, leaving the planet behind, and now discovering geological information from other sources.

It is a mistake to assume learning will be in clearly defined boxes, limited by designers of education material. Like the internet of today, the metaverse it likely to offer a continual intersectional experience of education, where facts, information and opinion don't run in straight lines, but rather in an enormous web of ever changing and moving information that can be accessed from any point within it.

In that sense, there is likely to be little separating the educational metaverse from the more general metaverse, unless some companies, universities or others attempt to put their knowledge, information, and data behind some kind of electronic wall.

Which brings us back to the question about how open source the metaverse is likely to become.

In the meantime, universities and corporations across the world have already shown extreme interest in virtual learning, sharing, and the expansion these methods offer.

In September 2020, NEOMA, a top-ranked business school in Paris, France, launched the first entirely virtual university campus in Europe.

The campus, situated on a virtual island, allows a personalized avatar to study as if they were on a real campus. They can take courses, attend classes, meet with fellow pupils, visit the career center, the library, and access break out rooms.[2]

FE News in the United Kingdom reports that two 'tech disruptor' companies, Credersi and PixelMax, had already spent over a year developing and creating their own virtual science and tech campus by the time Meta started talking about education and the metaverse.

"The Credersi World science and tech campus is an immersive experience with its own real estate. Delegates enter the concourse – much like they would at a physical university campus – and will be able to delve into different learning pods relevant to their courses. Various boulevards line the tech estate, which engages with the delegates at all levels, providing breakout rooms, libraries, shops, cinemas, art galleries, oceanic aquariums, as well as virtual banks and even well-being counsellors...

"The lecture boulevard will have rooms that allow delegates to wander in and listen to visiting academics and tech entrepreneurs giving masterclasses. Bio scientists will be able to carry out and conduct live experiments in AR and VR laboratories, while coders and cyber security students can simulate real-time ethical hacking and defense exercises on real life infrastructures."[3]

The benefits to universities are manifold. Not least because their pupils are able to learn and share education without the expense and risks, such as passing on Covid-19, associated with physical meetings. They will also be able to expand their reach further all over the world. In both the United States and across Europe, overseas students make up a significant income for universities. In the UK, the government restricts the amount home students pay for their university education. But for non-UK students, universities can charge a lot.

The metaverse is likely to introduce a world where different students can learn under the guise of a particular university, but pay different amounts, all without having to leave home. Set aside the benefits of leaving home to study, which are manifold, this model could well flatten access to high quality higher and further education for all.

Just like I can play Red Alert or Fortnite alongside someone living in the Philippines, I will be able to sit next to them in a virtual lecture theatre, converse with them - each of us speaking in our own language, translated by the metaverse - and learn equally. I need not even know their background, gender, nationality, or income group.

Korea Advanced Institute of Science and Technology (KAIST) in Daejeon, South Korea, is launching Kenya-KAIST by 2023.

The campus will be 60 km outside Nairobi, where the Korean university will "go beyond online education by creating a 'metaverse' that provides assistance for running classes and creates an immersive learning experience that runs the gamut of campus activities while using the latest digital technologies.

"Using online content there will help mitigate the educational gap between the two institutions, plus it will reduce the need for many students and faculty to make the long commute from the capital to the campus."[4]

In the metaverse, our traditional idea of static, long established universities owning and delivering information may well become out of date anyway. It can easily be envisaged that any individual learner could outsource their learning to any set of academic tutors, working on a freelance basis.

Imagine a world where students build their own academic courses by choosing modules on offer as easily as Amazon offers books, or eBay offers goods.

Learners can drill down through categories of the

subject matter they're most interested in, or which particular employers demand they study, do the course, engage with the tutors, achieve grades, and get certified for those modules. The idea of a single certifying university, or any need for a single university to host or govern a particular pupil's learning might become out of date.

On the flip side, universities may themselves reap the benefits of the metaverse at the expense of the individual professors and academics, by insisting on recording and owning lectures they deliver, then repacking them and presenting them through artificial intelligence in the metaverse. These technologies could allow for the production of an infinite number of lectures delivered by a range of animated and avatar academics in many, many languages, monetizing an individual's original academics lecture or theories for the university.

Platforms like Udemy and Future Learn, which offer buy-to-learn courses are already prolific. Not only can students or casual learners pay small amounts to access the courses, but anyone who believes they have knowledge, skills or expertise to share, can create their own courses, and sell them on the platform. Just like on Amazon, the content is clearly outlined before sale, and a sample is provided. Those who have taken the courses can rate them in terms of presentation, knowledge learned, quality of the course and materials, and value for money.

The university as we know it might become outdated in a metaverse where the learner becomes in charge of their own learning, picking and choosing providers, just as they would pick an evening's viewing on Netflix.

It has happened to shopping. It has happened to television. There is no reason to suspect the metaverse won't be the ideal platform for the same educational revolution to take place.

"Students may find that their learning can be paid for in a variety of new ways," writes John Preston, Economic and Social Research Council Leadership Fellow in Conflict, Crime and Security at Essex University UK. "This might be buying a virtual seat in a lecture hall with a particularly entertaining animated professor, converting a qualification earned in the virtual world into a real-world certificate or paying fees in bitcoin.

"Ultimately, the metaverse might result in the end of some traditional forms of university education. Rather than attending a single bricks-and-mortar institution, students might flock to the cyber-physical realm instead."

Workplace learning and training

These same principles will be applicable to the commercial world, where companies require their employees to take specific training in their own equipment, processes, and workplace culture. And, probably, an open market of training resources available to company employees on general working practices such as workplace health and safety, how to use particular Apps, self-improvement, and good posture.

It seems clear that the metaverse's virtual reality education space is seen as a live channel for investment. While some corporations and universities are interested in the delivery of education to schools, colleges, and universities, it seems delivery to the private sector offers much more scope.

Meta is investing heavily in this area. Facebook Reality Labs said it has invested $150 million in an education program to assist with tech development and to train people to use augmented and virtual reality tools.

Meta has also announced it is establishing its own curriculum to train people to use augmented and virtual reality in their workplace learning, which it calls the Spark AR Curriculum.

Companies that now routinely use VR for training employees include oil exploration companies BP and Exon, which both run immersive experiences to train platform workers about escape and emergency scenarios; the fast food chain Kentucky Fried Chicken has an 'escape room' virtual training program called The Hard Way to train new employees on how to cook the perfect breaded chicken (yes, Colonel Sanders barks orders and ideas at you during the simulation); UPS uses VR to teach drivers how to react to road hazards; and Walmart trains shopping assistants to deal with scenarios like Black Friday using VR.

Even the New York Police Department trains officers to deal with shootings on virtual reality, including a gun toter on the loose in a high school. All scenarios are based on real incidents. The system also allows the scenario to learn from the officers it trains. As more and more officers go through the training, they are able to model how a typical officer acts in a particular way, then that can influence what training is further needed for individuals, or whether whole new approaches to a scenario are required.

The metaverse will be a safe place to train for officers and indeed shop staff. Real life can provide the occasional opportunity for an officer to encounter a shooter, or a shop assistant to have to deal with a shelf falling. In VR, it can be practiced again and again, to discover the best case scenarios.

In conclusion, the metaverse is likely to be full of

opportunities for education and training, which not only develop the skills of employees and the capacity of universities and companies, but which also loop back into the metaverse to ever improve how education and training is delivered.

Take aways

- Children and young adults are already very comfortable with working in the virtual world, and are likely to lead adaption to the metaverse for all of us.
- Metaverse hardware and AI are likely to add value to children's learning experiences, but some think it won't be able to replace spontaneous learning.
- Commentators argue the metaverse should not be allowed to prevent regular personal interaction between pupils and real teachers.
- The metaverse may improve the university experience, by engaging access to information, experience, and opinion.
- Students may be able to build their own university courses, from modules offered around the world, to achieve qualifications.

HEALTH AND MEDICINE

If face-to-face contact with our doctors and medical professionals was on the wane because of pressures on their time and expertise at the start of this decade, it was forced to an absolute minimum by Covid-19.

Hospital entries through accident and emergency departments were drastically reduced. Patients were asked to use 911 and 999 services only in absolute emergencies. Our own doctors' surgeries asked us to stay away, or banned any face-to-face contact at all, reverting to telephone or Zoom calls.

It forced medical professionals and bodies from across the sector to invest in, or try out for the first time, remote practices and online contact.

We should not get ahead of ourselves. Covid-19 was appalling for patients experiencing the virus, but also for other patients. According to medical journal The Lancet, cancer diagnosis and treatment was severely affected across the higher income world, as patients didn't seek advice or treatment because they feared either getting Covid-19 or taking vital doctor time away from the pandemic.

"Around 40,000 fewer people than normal started cancer treatment in the UK last year, and US hospitals have been deluged by Covid-19 cases, rendering patients with cancer unable to obtain timely care. The World Health Organization has reported that one in three European countries had partially or completely interrupted cancer care services early in the pandemic. The UK's NHS currently has more than 4.6 million people on waiting lists for surgery and 300,000 people have been on hold for more than 12 months - a wait time that is 100 times higher than before the pandemic."[1]

But the same article credited the pandemic for huge medical advances, not only the successful rush to find a vaccination for Covid-19, but also the increased and improved inter-working between medical establishments, drugs companies, and governments to find solutions.

In total lockdown, a lot of this sharing work took place online, through sharing of data and information, and through online video conferencing.

It demonstrated what could be done on a local doctor scale, as well as what could be achieved in hospitals, the medical sector, and across governments and nations by using the most up to date technology.

If education is a driver of the metaverse, medicine and health are certainly co-drivers and definite beneficiaries.

The metaverse offers opportunities to improve personal health, the delivery of medical practices, and the development of new interventions.

"Industry stalwarts are investing billions of dollars in deciphering how augmented and virtual reality may allow for better, more personalized delivery of medicine, and possibly even mimic "physical presence," one of the key limitations to telehealth modalities currently," according to Sai Balasubramanian, M.D., in Forbes magazine.

Family medicine and health

Covid-19 has changed the way we contact and benefit from our personal family doctors.

The metaverse will build on our new experience of remote contact. We might, for example, be able to remotely book doctor's appointments, and then carry out initial appointments with a junior doctor's avatar. We might be able to take photographs, video, or live footage of any particular physical problem, or just talk to the junior doctor, who may assess our needs in a virtual reality space.

In virtual reality we *may* feel some level of the personal contact that many of us appreciate when we meet with our doctors. Once again, it will not mimic what takes place in the real world, but we might learn to appreciate the different experience. And we'll gain from reduced time traveling to a doctor's surgery and sitting in a waiting room.

Rather like we wait for deliveries, we could book a doctor's slot in hours, and then be brought into the surgery virtually any time in that hour, if convenient for us. We may then be able to get on with our home or work life, instead of feeling like we're wasting it. And doctors may be able to better manage their time.

Seeing a junior doctor, or an experienced nurse, in virtual reality will also offer an opportunity for triage. That is, the practice of separating patients who require intensive, expert help, and those who's complaint is more easily dealt with by a nurse, or advice center, or can be directed towards information elsewhere in the metaverse such as a pharmacist, a physiotherapist, or mental health expert.

In the metaverse, those contacts might be more seamless than they can be now, where we can virtually walk out of a doctor's surgery and directly into the pharmacy, the dentists or our local virtual club for people who just want someone to talk to.

In the meantime, the senior doctors may be able to work more efficiently, dealing with the most serious and emergency health cases. And doctors, nurses, and junior doctors can train online, again and again: trying out different virtual scenarios, perhaps even with artificial intelligence, with all the data from previous cases to hand, so they can model what great responses to their patients and their complaints might look like.

Such a version of the medicine metaverse might find patients are more accurately directed towards the kind of doctor they need. Instead of a general practitioner of medicine, who attempts to deal with the gamut of medical conditions as a first point of contact, we may be immediately transferred to a gynecologist, or pain consultant, or bloods specialist, or dermatologist, or mental health professional.

And AI could help those professionals identify more quickly, based on hundreds or thousands of previous cases, what the problem is most likely to be, and what might be the next best course of action.

Some might argue this metaverse medicine might lead to us treating our health as a shopping experience, rather like the university courses posited above. After all, do we want doctors or robots to diagnose our medical conditions?

Others, though, might appreciate it could lead to patients being able to get to a specialist or treatment more rapidly, or get the explanations and treatments that reassure them before their case even gets to doctor level.

What the metaverse might also provide, especially if we are able to attend virtual reality meetings, is the opportunity to get a clearer idea of what the problems we have are, or even look like on the inside. Imagine a virtual doctor being able to bring up a virtual version of a knee joint, rotate it and show where your kneecap isn't running across bones correctly. Even better, what if it was a virtual image of your own knee?

If you had a brain tumor or breast cancer, an oncologist or neurologist could swipe up a virtual version of your brain or breast, generated from your last MRI scan. They could take you 'physically' into tissue, showing you the specific areas that are being affected, and what they expect treatment to achieve in terms of reduction.

Surely all this is better than the jargon many of us experience when we talk to expert doctors.

Medical care in the metaverse will not be the same as physical contact. During Covid-19, Zoom calls and telephone calls have led to faster satisfaction for some, but frustrations for others who don't feel the doctor 'cares' in the way they would face-to-face.

Doctors get to know families. Individually, and as a group of doctors in a community, they get to know those in their areas. They watch our kids grow up, they know our complaints, our tendencies. They may know our problems and lifestyles more intimately than the rest of our families. Questions remain about whether this intimate relationship with our doctors could be retained in a virtual world, using avatars or even video calls.

It is well known that doctors read non-verbal signs about their patients' well-being and pain levels; they are charged also with identifying unspoken issues such as domestic violence, depression, or financial crises. Notoriously, doctors know that the complaints patients come to their appointments with are often not what the patients are really seeking help for.

Many question whether this can be replicated in the metaverse, with most - including medical practitioners - doubting it can.

Which brings the issue back to what benefit digitizing the medical relationship would have for patients, in view of the alternative. Just because the metaverse will exist, doesn't mean we have to carry out every aspect of our life within it.

As Sai Balasubramanian concludes in Forbes magazine: "Finally, just because it can be done, the question remains—should it? ... Perhaps there are incredible benefits to be gained from this. But, if it isn't done correctly, it may also pose a threat to the personalized nature of the patient-physician relationship. Indeed, amidst a push to embrace new innovation and technology, society cannot afford to lose the humanistic touch of healthcare."[2]

It is also worth noting that if the future vision for the metaverse is realised, then all comers may be able to enter the virtual space and set up their own practices, shops, consultancies, and services.

This means there are likely to be a proliferation - just like there are now on the internet, Facebook and YouTube - of wellness gurus and practitioners, scam artists, false cure pushers, and natural health advisors, as well as anti-vaccination and anti-medical establishment advocates who will emerge in the metaverse space.

It can and will be the duty of patients themselves to make sound judgements about what they accept as truth and what they are willing to risk, but there will also be a question about what role metaverse companies, as well as governments, should have in regulating medicine, and those who claim to offer medicine. And a further question about how consistent this regulation can be on a global platform.

For example, in the United Kingdom, it is illegal to promote a cure for cancer that has not been scientifically proven. But there is nothing to prevent British people viewing YouTube videos that profess all kinds of cures without proof, nor traveling to countries which are not so strict, to receive untested and unproven treatments.

If a practitioner sets up their own independent 'clinic' in the metaverse, and promotes their cures, or methods, how will that be regulated? In fact, how will medicine in general, over such a wide range, with different rules in different countries, be managed?

Issues covering sexual health, abortion, right-to-die, even medication may come to the forefront in a world that is not government by borders, but by our internet connections.

Personal fitness and exercise

According to statistics agency Statista, India and Sweden top the charts when it comes to ownership of wearable smart devices with 45% of households, with China coming in at 42%, and the UK and the US at 40%.

Whether we're counting steps, recording our runs or cycle rides, or measuring our heartbeat, our use of mobile devices to manage our health is ever increasing. And so is our posting of that data online, and carrying out some of the exercise we're recording in the online and virtual space.

Back in 2006, we were playing our kids at tennis, and doing step ups and dance workouts on Nintendo Wii Sport.

At 8.3 million copies, Wii Sport was the fourth biggest selling computer game of all time. (Though easily dwarfed by Minecraft at nearly 24 million.)

Even before then, some of us were hitting golf balls against a canvas screen and watching an image of the ball run off into the distance onto a faraway 3D rendered green.

It's not hard to see how the metaverse is likely to be a central place for us to share exercise, share our data, learn how to improve our fitness and exercise disciplines, and hold ourselves accountable for our progress.

Even before Covid-19, Zwift had become a primary program for cyclists, including pro-cyclists, to train or exercise on static bikes. Cyclists set up their mobile devices, screens or large TVs, and ride virtual rides, in 3D. Since then there have been many competitors, including Peloton.

Zwift works by uniting software and hardware to allow the avatar of the rider to go faster or slower, move forward, left or right. When a hill appears on the virtual screen, the training hardware makes it harder to pedal, when going downhill it becomes easier.

Cyclists can ride alone, or with friends, or join races, competitions, frequent (like every minute or so) group rides with other cyclists from around the world, and work towards achieving long miles, average speeds, climbing goals or any other target. And as well as virtual prizes like badges, participants can also earn real money, merchandise, and sponsored goods.

And of course, all the data is stored, then can be shared. A rider can see their 'rank' in their own club, or on a particular stretch, or worldwide if that's what they want. Riders can even compete with professional cyclists, some of whom are paid by Zwift to participate.

This kind of experience is just the beginning of what the

metaverse is likely to offer. Zwift is currently a 3D, flat-screen experience. Riders see other riders, and can choose their particular view-point, including an overview of the route they're taking. By leaning or selecting, they can choose routes. Zwift has now expanded to running, allowing training on static running machines.

In the metaverse, imagine this experience moving into a virtual dimension. Instead of selecting between a choice of relatively static viewpoints, a ride could look to the side, or even over their shoulder, and see in real time the riders accompanying them.

They could see themselves from the side, or front. If selected, they could share data about their heartbeat, sweat levels, even a real or digital representation of the pain on their face. Making the experience as real as possible, only with the ability to share the experience in real time across the world.

In the metaverse, without leaving our homes, we could receive one-to-one training on our exercise disciplines, not only on fitness but in technique too. A combination of virtual reality and artificial intelligence could record everything from distance cycled to heart rate, blood sugar levels, to body fat and mental concentration. It may use this information to tailor exact exercise regimes for each individual.

With body sensors, pressure gloves and slimmed down VR headsets, we could do anything from karate to Pilates, boxing to baton twirling.

With as-yet undeveloped software and hardware, we will be able to play team sports in our own gardens, or if we take our smart devices and headsets to our nearest green spaces.

Once again, all measured, data captured, and shared in real time. The computer gaming world is rapidly pursuing these immersive competitive worlds and profiting from serious sponsorship deals. There's no reason why sport and exercise won't ride on the coat tails.

There will also be opportunities for us to benefit from AI in the metaverse exercise world. One can imagine attending a yoga class in the metaverse, with a teacher at the 'front' of a class of ten, or 100, or even 1,000 other participants. For each participant, we might enjoy the attention of an AI robot that helps us to correct our own specific position, or advises us to stretch more, or when a position might be too difficult for us.

If the AI is pre-programmed with the correct position, the individual attention from a teacher would not be required, just the demonstration and motivation. Perhaps even that will be a luxury once a yoga teacher has created their course. Theoretically, they could allow AI to run the course from then on, over and over and over again, to many thousands of participants over long periods of time.

We could even get to a point where AI is learning yoga from other's videos or classes, then going on to design and deliver yoga classes without any human instruction whatsoever. We could also get to a place where doctors are routinely prescribing VR workouts for particular conditions.

If that seems far-fetched, it's worth reminding ourselves that ten years ago few would have imagined cycling, rowing, or running against other competitors, without leaving a single spot in our basement or garage.

And this could also be where our exercise, our online and our real lives find another conjunction. Health insurance companies currently offer bonuses of gym membership for their subscribers, even going so far as to keep premiums low for those who exercise regularly (proof of frequent gym attendance required).

We could see this extended in the metaverse. Health insurance benefits offered for any kind of exercise carried out in the metaverse. Perhaps discounts from health food stores, depending on the miles someone runs or cycles. Money off new sneakers, if you reach 10,000 steps a day for ten days. The options are endless, and all we need do is share our data. Which many of us are happy to do now, but what if the implications went deeper?

Should governments be allowed to assess someone's exercise levels, before judging whether they should receive health benefits, for example? Will private companies and organizations insist on seeing our exercise patterns and health records, before considering someone for employment?

Suddenly, the metaverse becomes a place where we're encouraged and motivated to exercise, but actually pay to do so through the exchange of data. That might not do us many favors. It might even prejudice those who don't post their data, or choose not to do exercise in the metaverse. No-one expects that from a jog in the park.

There also remains the question of being realistic about exercise and the metaverse. In his interview with TheVerge, Mark Zuckerberg envisages a metaverse where "you feel present with other people as if you were in other places, having different experiences that you couldn't necessarily do on a 2D App or webpage, like dancing, for example, or different types of fitness."

In his launch video of Meta, he says you'd simply need your VR headset. The video then goes on to show a pumped up woman flinging herself around a boxing ring, against an AI adversary, which looks half-balloon half-robot. Then it cuts to six people playing basketball, each person playing 'on the other side of the world'. Finally, Mark himself fences with Olympic Gold Medallist Lee Kiefer, and is out of breath at the end. They played for about five seconds.

Really? The difficulty with all of the above is that they are heavy duty, sweaty, high intensity sports.

As they currently are, no-one is going to be convinced it is worth wearing a heavy, clumsy VR headset to join in, no matter how many friends you get to play basketball with from across the world.

Even if those goggles develop (Zuckerberg promises sweat-resistant accessories), we will still be in our heated homes, small spaces (compared with basketball pitches), and be surrounded by kids, dogs, furniture which we won't be able to see because... we're wearing full VR headsets.

"And that's what fitness will be like in the metaverse," says Zuckerberg.

Well, in that case it needs to be better. Because none of this will *really* involve pulling on a headset and you're ready to go. Static cycling and running requires expensive kit, let alone a high powered fan to keep you cool while exercising indoors. Indoor basketball is surely going to need a high ceiling indoors, or a very good internet connection outdoors. If a user has any outdoors of their own to play on.

And if you and a few friends are playing using immersive headsets on a park or open space, who's looking after your stuff? Who's ensuring you're all safe from being attacked by a dog, or by someone who just fancies their own Oculus headset?

One would suspect many would prefer to actually be on a pitch, or outside, using a real ball and their real eyes. As fun as riding on Zwift can be, there are few cyclists who would prefer it to riding outside.

In the metaverse sector, there does seem to be a dose of 'book it and they will come' mentality, but as exciting as the new technology is, it won't last the test of time in fitness and exercise unless it is enjoyable and preferable to just getting out and doing your fitness work without it.

This feels like a very long way off.

Professional medicine

This is where the metaverse will come into its own, for the benefit of medicine in general and for patients across the world.

It breaks down into general principles in medicine, which are already deeply ingrained in the kind of information sharing that the metaverse will build upon. Medical training and development; the sharing of cases and information; and augmented reality treatment.

Like in any aspect of the metaverse, this will bring challenges. Not least, the question of privacy and our right to protect our own medical information.

Training

From earliest times, images of bodies and the dissection of bodies have been key to the best training of medics: from doctors and oncologists, to nurses, dentists and more. From ancient Egyptian papyri charting the internal organs of dead bodies, to 3D rendering on flat screens of brains in the 21st century, imagery has always been medicine's best friend.

Today, junior doctors can be trained in particular illnesses by looking at 3D images, and using flat screens, they can enjoy 360 degree views of body parts at various stages of illness. In the metaverse, this is likely to become yet more effective, with students able to use their hands or medical tools to go deeper into a particular organ, separate its parts, and see in real time what they have been taught.

With AI, or pre-programed scenarios, they may be able to carry out actions - add a drug, stop a blood flow - and watch in real time the results of their actions. They will be learning on the job, but with no risk to patients.

In surgery, this will be of particular use. One can envisage surgeons carrying out very detailed 'operations' on virtual reality patients, every action recorded with the later ability to revisit and understand what they did right, wrong, or might have done more efficiently. And once a set-up is in place, it can be carried out again and again, without the need for living (or deceased) patients for surgeons to practice on.

One can also envisage a real life surgery of a regular kind, say a hip replacement, carried out in real life, but filmed in very high resolution from a number of angles. This data could be recreated digitally in the metaverse, and then used as a future practice model for other surgeons to learn from and imitate.

Taken one step forward, a doctor might be able to practice for a single particular complex operation, say brain surgery, using virtual reality. Once that operation is pinned down as good as it could be, the learning and data could be transferred to the real world. The doctor might then use augmented reality - a mix of real life, and virtual reality - to carry out the operation, accompanied by AI assistants, even robots, ready with sutures, needles, and anything else the doctor has previously needed in the metaverse practice scenarios.

Miniature robotics are already used in very complex surgery cases. With the future development of AI, physical robotics, and scenario modeling, it is possible that the metaverse may breed scenarios where AI enabled robots may carry out medical operations themselves, with surgeons only overseeing what is taking place.

But decent metaverse training may not be confined to training for physical procedures. Doctors are already required to carry out online surveys about how they should respond to their patients, their families, and loved ones. How much information to share; how to judge the knowledge level of patients; how to show empathy. Though lots of surgeons don't like this kind of work, they have to do it to show they are real people.

How much easier might it be if medical professionals go through AI training in the metaverse, where AI avatars are programmed to respond in different ways to news about their loved one's treatment? Again, the doctors could learn the best ways in certain scenarios, and afterwards go through their responses to see what could have been done better.

Most would argue that creating these 'real life' scenarios will be far more effective than simply rating what you might do on a scale of 1 to 5, or from a very happy face to a very sad one.

The result may be higher satisfaction with work for doctors, and among patients and their families.

It is also worth considering how AI and the metaverse might allow hospitals to prepare for crisis scenarios, such as a slow build up of critical cases due to a rapidly spreading virus, or a single emergency event such as a train crash.

Computer modeling will be able to create a practice scenario in which all staff and volunteers at a hospital have a role to play. Their natural reactions to situations could be recorded, AI could respond naturally (and randomly), and by the end of the situation, analysis could be made about how the hospital responded to the crisis.

This 'gaming' of scenarios is already regularly run in the military. With the help of the metaverse, it could very easily be rolled out in different situations like hospitals. Indeed, such modeling would also be perfect for schools, concerts, busy shopping centers, even on cruise ships. It might be envisaged that insurers *demand* this kind of modeling in order to offer lower premiums.

The question remains as to whether this will be regarded as satisfactory progress in the medical world. How far are we, for example, from patients only being able to converse with robots about their conditions, and never meeting surgeons or specialists at all? And surgeons feel they are working, instead, on some kind of factory line of patients that need the same procedure.

Again, will doctors or patients want these developments to take place? Most would need to be convinced of the benefits, and cost saving is unlikely to do the job.

Information sharing

Sharing data is central to how the medical establishment works today, which makes it an ideal area to benefit from the metaverse.

The benefits of constant data and idea exchange, as well as debate and discussion, can only improve medical decision making. This can be envisioned on the smallest scale, right up to a global level.

On a patient level, the metaverse may enable doctors and their patients to maintain a constant relationship. A patient might be prescribed to wear a smart watch or heart monitor, for example, or a device that takes regular blood pressure or blood samples. The data would be fed back to the consultant in real time, managed by AI.

The doctor would be notified if the patient's bloods or heartbeat was unusual, or not as excepted. At online meetings, these changes could be discussed, and medicine and prescriptions changed to account for them, using graphs and images illustrating patterns recorded.

In the same way, emergency services would be notified in relevant cases automatically. The stopping of heartbeats. Dangerously high or low blood pressure. Or too much or too little blood sugar.

On a slightly bigger scale, doctors already work in clinical medical teams, on the basis that two (or more) professional educated heads are better than one. Especially in chronic conditions and in cancer, doctors may discuss their caseloads with others in regular clinical case teams.

Prior to Covid-19, these would take place in large meeting rooms, with various experts offering their opinions and recommendations for each case. These meetings moved online during the pandemic, allowing consultants to work from home or without having to travel between hospitals. It also allowed wider consultation with specialists brought in to discuss particular cases.

In the metaverse, this tendency is likely to increase, once again improving the outcomes for patients. One can imagine very specialist clinical medical teams being established, for very specific conditions, which meet weekly to discuss their cases.

For example, there are around a dozen overall types of breast cancer, but within each of those types, there are multiple forms, and they are further delineated by the genetic makeup of the cancers.

In any one hospital or area, there might be two or three

cases at a time of a particular breast cancer of a particular form, with a particular genetic makeup. The oncologist would currently only have a small number of colleagues to consult with, who may not be specialists in that particular cancer type, or even breast cancer at all.

The metaverse might flip this on its head. Clinical medical teams could be established across the globe, bringing together world experts in that particular breast cancer, of that particular form, with that genetic signature. While there must be room for the unexpected, and for an outside view, it would be hard to argue that such specialist case attention would not be beneficial to patients.

In a practical sense, we might imagine a global sharing hospital in the metaverse, which has ongoing clinical medical team meetings at any one time. Consultants might be able to enter a particular room - *breast cancer, ductal carcinoma in situ* - and present their case, or just watch and listen in to the latest cases being presented from all over the world.

Imagine now if surgeons and oncologists from the lower and middle-income world had easy access to this ongoing research and discussion. There are no limits in the metaverse on the number of attendances in a 'room' nor much cost involved, compared with traveling for a conference and taking time out from hospital duties.

Developments in medical practices in the higher income world would more quickly trickle across to the lower and middle-income world, and in turn new ideas and lessons may be learned in the higher income world from the particular situations experienced in the lower and middle-income world.

Which brings us to the larger scale information sharing that will be of benefit to medicine. The sharing of medical research is at the heart of the global medical establishment. This has traditionally been done through research papers, published as drafts in journals, and then reviewed and criticized, before being finalized and republished.

This peer review process is open, and vital for medical research to progress in the safest way. Researchers then gather together multiple research papers on the same wide topic, and drill down key conclusions, to present overviews. Those overviews are again peer reviewed. The resulting research is razor sharp, and becomes medical practice or advice.

This kind of research process is followed in everything from drug development to surgery techniques, treatment protocols, or patient-doctor relationships.

In the same way, there are daily medical conferences all over the world on very specific medical subjects. Practitioners and experts gather to present their latest research to other doctors and experts, where they face criticism, discussion, and new avenues for research are explored.

In London, UK, on the day of writing, there are professional medical conferences on: eye drugs, health and inactivity, pharmaceutical communications, patient safety culture, biological evaluation of medical devices, acting on patient experience, and professional development. Tomorrow, there are a similar number of conferences. In every major city in the higher income world, the same kind of conferences will be taking place every single day.

Naturally, these conferences take time and money to attend, but are vital to ongoing medical developments. Now imagine that whole sector gradually moves into the virtual space, via the metaverse.

First, it will be far more cost efficient and convenient for medical professional to attend conferences on their specialities, without having to travel away. They will be able to attend international events, sharing medical learning globally.

Secondly, the content they deliver or receive could be far richer than that enabled only by attending a conference physically. There could be more presentations at a metaverse medical conference than can be squeezed into a single venue, and a doctor could attend any of them, in any order. Starting perhaps with the ones they have something to contribute to, then to recorded ones that have taken place in another 'room' or among a special interest group.

Attendees will be able to view virtual presentations, including virtual renditions of models, body parts, DNA, drugs molecules. They will be able to discuss them in real time, using their avatars gathered together around the virtual image.

They will be able to view the paper being presented and add notes to it in real time. Post questions to panels and gather as much information as they need.

As with any conference, there would be specific social and networking events, so attendees can share information more informally, meet new people, and create ideas and partnerships for future research.

And vitally, thanks to AI, they will be able to engage with the conference in their own language, while other participants are doing the same in theirs. In the metaverse, these interactions will be seamless.

After the event, all videos, interactions, models, papers, in fact the whole conference will continue to exist. A consultant could attend the event a week later, if they liked, with lots of the same experiences.

Without the need for physical presence, or co-ordinated

timetables, the metaverse might present a completely alternative way to run and attend conference of all types. Just because we have previously experienced physical presence and time passing in conferences previously, doesn't mean that has to happen in the future.

Zoom, Microsoft Teams, Facebook, YouTube, and platforms like Google Docs, have already encouraged us to share data in a different, real time and collaborative way. It is easy to see how the metaverse will build on these platforms, to enable sharing of information in a completely new, probably more useful way still.

Privacy and ownership

Without adequate privacy protections, moving through this virtual space will be "kind of like having a drone following you around in real life, monitoring everything you do, and then passing that information on to whoever." So says psychologist Albert Rizzo, Director for Medical Virtual Reality at the University of Southern California's Institute for Creative Technologies on the Politico website.

If the metaverse is envisaged as a place where a doctor can measure and monitor our vital signs through smart watches, and that consultants can share digital information about us, including attending virtual meetings at which our details are discussed, there is a real danger that that information can 'leak'.

In its mildest forms, such information might become available to insurers, or social security offices, or police, influencing the way we are treated by them.

If social media companies are processing that data, there's little reason to believe that data won't be used to segment us into advertising categories, which medical companies and others can exploit to sell their goods.

Companies may promise that personal data won't be shared, but acres of health data analyzed more generally will be a gold mine in the metaverse, and it's hard to believe this won't be exploited.

Besides, the data will travel, and it needs to be stored. That will open it up, at least, to the danger of being stolen by cybercriminals. Platforms including Facebook, Twitter, WhatsApp, Twitch, and Apple have all been hacked in the last few years, as have numerous credit card platforms.

There is also the question of ownership of health data. To move around in the metaverse, and if we want to achieve good likeness in our avatars, we will need to share biometric data. Our height, body shape, weight, eye color and more. Much more, if we take into account opportunities health insurers might offer us in exchange for more data about our fitness.

That data belongs to us, right now. But if we share it on the metaverse, there remains a question of who *then* owns that information. If I create an avatar, does that avatar belong to me, in a copyright sense? Or does it belong to the metaverse platform in which I created the avatar?

Will I have to 'buy' the rights to my avatar, if I want to use it in a different context? Likewise, does my personal health and wellbeing information, once I've shared it in the metaverse - albeit with a legitimate doctor - remain my property, or is that data transferred to the platform on which I've shared it? If yes, then couldn't they sell that data in whatever guise they like.

Even more concerning is if AI processes an individual's data, and is 'clever' enough to create inferences from a person's data, to create new data about them. Who would now own that new data? My privacy isn't being breached, because the first level of data isn't being shared. But the new data, inferred from my medical records, may well be shared and there's nothing I can do about it.

Imagine if I suffered from depression. A metaverse company may be able to use that data, without sharing my diagnosis, to infer I suffer from anxiety, or that I take anti-depressant medication, or that I'm undergoing some kind of therapy. This isn't recorded in the data anywhere, but the processing of millions of other's data with depression and anti-depressants linked, might allow the AI to assume this to be the case.

New data about my medical condition is inferred. It may not be 100% correct, but with enough data to compare it to, a metaverse company might bank on 80%. Certainly high enough to be able to sell that data, in the same way as Amazon tracks someone who regularly buys kids' books, and assumes they have kids and offers them other books and shopping for kids.

Sandra Wachter, an associate professor at the Oxford Internet Institute at the University of Oxford, UK, is urging courts and lawmakers to get ahead of the development of the metaverse to ensure inferred data like this is protected, calling for regulators to put limits on how far companies interpret users' data for commercial ends - something many people are unaware of.

"They think it's a convenient thing that they, for free, get the ability to talk to their friends and families," she told Reuters. "Data collection just runs in the background. And you don't actually know that you're revealing your diary to the whole world".

Take aways

- Covid-19 illustrated what working virtually could achieve, in short amounts of time, in the medical world.
- Family doctors may benefit from metaverse-based interaction with patients, but it cannot replace face-to-face.
- AI may help doctors, researchers and medical practitioners learn, improve upon, and model medical knowledge.
- The metaverse may provide opportunities for exercise, leisure, and data sharing that may benefit some, but exclude others.
- Health and medicine in the metaverse raises serious questions about data and ownership of personal medical information.

SHOPPING

The retail guru Doug Stephens writes about the metaverse and shopping on the Business of Fashion website:

> "When it comes to retail, there are those that foresee the creation of shopping venues — stores, malls and more — in the metaverse. This is probably short-sighted. To simply transport industrial age shopping concepts and conventions to the metaverse would be both unimaginative and ineffective. The creation of the metaverse will allow us to break free from the current industrial form and function of physical stores and move light years beyond even the best digital shopping experiences of today."

This is a vital key point about the metaverse, that is easily missed. Doing most things in the metaverse will not attempt to mirror what goes on in the real world. Indeed, to do so might be a mistake.

What will shopping look like?

Shoppers, gamers, families, workers, and more may be turning to the metaverse for a new, different, more convenient, entertaining, or innovative way of doing things. Otherwise, why bother to use the metaverse at all?

To that end, it is a mistake to think that there will be malls and shopping centers as we know them in the mature metaverse. Brands, big and small, won't just open virtual versions of their physical shops, because there would be no added value.

Just as shopping has moved more recently from something we do because we need to, towards something more experiential - we're looking to enjoy shopping, to be entertained by it, to find it exciting - we'll be looking to the metaverse to offer something more experiential yet again.

Going into a virtual store to see a virtual coat rail, full of virtual clothes, then order them for delivery may seem exciting at first, but we're very likely to soon get bored and go back to the shopping mall, where we can get a coffee between shops.

Shopping in the metaverse will look different. It will be something we intensely experience before parting with our virtual currency.

"Why would one create a virtual replica of a Canada Goose store when in the metaverse I could potentially shop for a new Canada Goose coat from inside an Arctic exploration experience led by Iditarod [sled race] champion and Canada Goose spokesperson Lance Mackey?" asks Doug Stephens.

Take book shopping. Imagine walking into a virtual book shop, and immediately before you appear the kinds of books you already like - hovering in the air. You choose a particular book, and flick through it. In real virtual time, you can see the book in your hands, read the words, flip it over read the back cover, and if you have the right hardware, you'll feel the weight of the book in your hands.

When you look up, the stack of books you will have initially seen will have been replaced. Running across the shelf before you will be other books by the same author. If you turn to the left, there will be other books in the same specific genre as the book you're holding - horror, or medieval romance, or sci-fi end-of-the-world dystopian. If you turn to the right, you'll see books others have read that have highly rated the book you're holding.

You can blow all these books away with the swipe of a hand, and speak a command asking the bookshop to search up a particular title, a particular genre, or a particular issue. You'll be presented with the best sellers, the recommendations, and the paid-for advertising for a new series of books.

All very exciting, right?

It is also very out of date.

In a 2D way, Amazon and similar online bookstores already offer us exactly this experience. Every visit we make is specifically tailored to our needs, and programmed by algorithms to ensure we go through and buy the products we're browsing. Adding a physical experience won't add too much to something that already exists.

In 2021, I wrote a book called *Future Shop* mirroring this scenario, with my lead character visiting a supermarket. Just like the bookshop above, she was offered the products the algorithms knew she liked, and was bombarded with other offers that were like her purchases, which she ended up buying. I shan't share the ending, but it didn't turn out as well as she thought it would. I hope you'll read it. I started this book in a similar way, because to plunge right in would have been confusing.

But as I've learned more about the metaverse, it's become clear that shopping won't be like what I've suggested. We might visit bookshops and supermarkets in this way, but we will also do something very different.

We will buy on the fly.

Imagine simply walking down a virtual street in the metaverse. You see someone wearing a funky pair of virtual jeans. You might look at those jeans and call out 'shop'. Along the bottom of your virtual experience, you'll be presented with a selection of jeans from the 'virtual shop' where these digital versions came from, exactly sized to your own body.

In a moment, you'll be able to swipe through the various versions of the same jeans, select the pair you like most, virtually lift them into a shopping basket, which will automatically process your payment in Metacoin. You can select for your avatar to wear them, or for those jeans to be delivered to your real self in real life.

Or both.

And you'll even be able to try on these jeans in the metaverse, to see what you look like. No-one will notice, even if they're walking down the street with you, as your avatar won't show you're trying on the jeans (unless you want them to!).

Once you've bought the jeans, you'll carry on down the street, on the way to your virtual workplace, or wherever. You never entered a shop. You weren't considering new jeans. You were not even shopping.

"Oh, we need coffee beans," you say out loud as you're sitting at your virtual desk. Consider them bought. That's not shopping. But it sure is convenient.

Just as retailers will pay for virtual retail space in the metaverse, they're just as likely - or even more likely - to pay platforms to enable, or even promote their goods to be bought in this way.

More specifically, they may arrange for their goods to be shown only to a target audience in the metaverse. This is exactly what happens on Facebook and Amazon right now.

Gary is a cyclist. As he rides down the virtual high street on his virtual bike, mirroring the real ride he's currently doing in his garage, there might be various cycling paraphernalia, accessories and more cycling goods rendered in 3D along his route. He can pick these up, examine them, then discard them, all without stopping his bike ride. The things he wants, or would like to consider more, he can drop into a basket.

Like a race car game of today, he can literally pimp his ride as he goes along.

Now take Stephanie. She plays rugby, and is also walking down the same street as Gary is riding down. To her, the goods on offer are completely different. Rugby boots, mouth guards, clothing, sweat bands, head protectors. She doesn't see any cycling stuff, because she's not interested in cycling. Just as Gary doesn't see any rugby stuff.

Now let's say Gary and Stephanie are romantic partners, and the metaverse knows this. Come Gary's birthday, and with his permission, there's no reason why Stephanie shouldn't be able to see the cycling gear Gary has shown most interest in lately, but not quite bought. That's Gary's birthday gift sorted this year.

Very quickly, the whole of the metaverse will be a shopping experience, with the opportunity to buy anything around you that you see, or anything you can call up as you're walking around in the virtual world.

Just as on most current social media platforms, retailers will aim advertising directly at you and pay for each 'click'. The offers, billboards, free stuff, clothing on artificially intelligent robots, even the shops you pass, will appear only because it is *you* that are looking at them. For the person who lives with you, the metaverse will look entirely different. For your next door neighbor, it'll look different again. Kids' metaverses will be full of kids' stuff. Dog owners' metaverses will be offered dog stuff. Non-doggy people won't get a whiff of it.

And for every advert we see in the metaverse, it won't be a 'brand awareness' exercise, like much advertising is in the real world. It will be fully interactive. We'll be able to swipe the advert for a theme park that appears on the side of a virtual bus (because the metaverse knows we like theme parks) and be taken immediately to that theme park for a free go on any virtual ride we like, and take away with us a discount code for our first booking. A friend likes museums, and the advert she sees on the same bus is for the national museum. She can swipe and immediately find herself in the dinosaur exhibition.

In this way, shopping in the metaverse is far from 3D or even virtual. It is many multi-layers of interacted webs of algorithms, creating a unique experience based on our previously expressed desires and preferences, and our data and how much retailers are willing to spend in an auction competition to get our attention. Just as exactly happens on Facebook, Amazon and everywhere else in social media.

Shopping is a good place to illustrate this, but the same principles apply across the metaverse in everything we have so far touched on, and will go on to learn about.

Shopping in the virtual world

What we are also likely to see is the growth of metaverse-only goods. Once again, it is a mistake to imagine the virtual internet of tomorrow is going to simply mirror the goods and experiences we have in real life.

Instead, we can expect an increasing market of goods that only exist in the metaverse. And with that, a market of goods that don't make sense outside of it.

The first is easier to explain. In the real world, most people do not own and fly airplanes. Generally, we don't own and run football or baseball teams. Most don't have twenty fast race cars, in our own branded colors, nor own buildings which we build with our own hands.

In the metaverse, all of these things are perfectly possible. We'll buy virtual planes, and be able to fly them using just our VR headsets and some controls. We can already manage football, baseball, cycling, hockey, and any other kind of teams in gaming software, and this will transfer easily to the metaverse. Our kids can set up teams, our partners can set up teams, and we can create and run as many leagues as we like, playing against each other or strangers on the internet. My son has a whole city of his own in Minecraft.

The nature of the metaverse is that it is infinite, there will be no restriction on 'space' as we traditionally know it. You want a spaceship? Go ahead and draw one, and get your kids to make one. Boom, time for take-off.

In the metaverse, there will be a retail world that is more than happy for us to achieve these very real dreams. We can buy advice, virtual raw materials, creative services, design, and build space to race our F1 cars. And we can sell our own skills and expertise too, in one huge and unlimited marketplace.

The second, is more difficult to explain and understand. There may be goods we want in the metaverse that don't actually exist in the real world, that only exist in the metaverse, and which makes no sense to exist in the real world and certainly would have no value here.

For example, we might be able to create, or buy, a true anti-gravity machine. In the real world, zero gravity is mimicked on earth. It isn't real. But in a wholly digital world, anything is possible. We may be able to step into an anti-gravity machine, and no longer be subjected to the (virtual) law of gravity in the virtual world. Assuming those laws apply in the virtual world at all.

We may be able to build our own planets, bigger than the earth, because all that needs is the right computer code implemented in a virtual space. We can go and live on that planet, which we can code to have all the wonderful things we want. A sun that shines brightly, but does not burn our skin. An ecosystem that is endless, and cannot be destroyed by our digital pollutants.

We may be able to literally code into the metaverse contradictions to the real world we live in, that don't obey the rules we were taught at school.

Once we get that concept, we can bring it down to a plain retail level: a shoe shop will design and sell shoes to us in the metaverse which are designed only for us and which only we can wear, that never wear out and which allow us to jump higher than is possible in the real world.

We will be able attend a virtual concert, in which we always get one of the unlimited front row seats. We may be able to buy bricks made of jello and build a house with them that cannot fall down.

We may be able to build an avatar of ourselves that never wears out, never gets tired, and if involved in a negative event, always recovers, shows no injury, or just rejuvenates itself like PacMan used to every time he was caught by those pesky ghosts.

We may be able to buy, exchange, sell, and manufacture things that you and I have never even considered would exist in the real world, or even in a virtual reality. And with the powers of design, creation, ingenuity, and sheer glee of innovation, retailers and businesses will tumble over themselves, and others, to invent and provide goods that we never knew we wanted, but in ten years' time we daren't be without.

Imagine 40 years ago, a physical store in a mall attempting to sell us a broadband connection. We wouldn't have a clue what the shop assistant was going on about. Now think about 40 years into the future, and what retailers in the (as yet untrodden) metaverse might be selling.

And we'll lap it all up, just like everyone reading this has their own 4G or 5G mobile device, they just can't possibly be without.

Imagine a metaverse without a fligabonda, we'll say. Gosh, Dad, did you really not have a fligabonda when you were young? You must be so ancient; I've already got three fligabonda and want more.

We have already discussed blockchains and non-fungible assets in the finance section of this book. These are likely to come further to the fore in every shopping experience we have, particularly when we are buying clothes, experiences, vehicles, flashy gear, fligabonda, or whatever for our metaverse avatars.

We could pick a GAP T-shirt from someone we've walked past in the metaverse. We ask to look at that T-shirt in more detail, and discover that particular design, in that color, is wholly owned by that particular avatar. It is that avatar's non fungible asset. It cannot be reproduced; it cannot be copied.

But we still like that GAP T-shirt, so go into the virtual GAP store (or more like, call it to us) and we're able to design our own, or pick another T-shirt we like so much, that we want to ensure that no-one else in the whole metaverse can own that T-shirt. We buy it as a non-fungible asset. It'll cost more than a more 'general' plain T-shirt at GAP, but we're paying for the experience of being the only one in the world, real- or meta-, to actually own it.

Or if we're so keen on that other avatar's T-shirt, and we have the virtual currency, well we can simply offer that avatar Metacoin to buy it from them. Now we own the GAP T-shirt, he goes back to a plain T-shirt some Metacoin richer. Everyone wins.

And you thought shopping in the metaverse was going to be less stressful that a trip to Walmart.

Take aways

- It might be a mistake to think the metaverse intends to mirror the real world, it will be very different.
- Shopping may not take place in 'virtual shops' but merely as we are living our lives.
- Retailers may be able to super-target their goods

to us depending on our demographics and previous behavior in the metaverse.

- We will be able to buy metaverse-only goods, such as football teams, images, designs, and property that don't exist in the real world.
- There may be opportunities to create goods in the metaverse that could not exist in the real world, such as items and experiences that don't obey the laws of physics.

SOCIAL MEDIA, LEISURE, AND GAMING

It is interesting to note that in his launch video of Meta, and in his interview with TheVerge, Mark Zuckerberg announces that, "I think we will effectively transition from people seeing us as primarily being a social media company to being a metaverse company."

This might well seem perverse at first glance. Surely, the metaverse will depend on social media: isn't the metaverse actually the conglomeration of all the ways we communicate, broadcast, sell and buy online, and share information?

Social media companies are at the height of their powers right now. Out of the following, how many do you have an account with: Facebook, Instagram, WhatsApp, Google Apps, FaceTime, Twitter, LinkedIn, Tumblr, Pinterest, Reddit, TikTok, Flickr, NextDoor, Tinder, and MySpace?

Surely all of these functions are going to play a key role in the development and the population of the metaverse? This assumption may well be mistaken.

Social media

These social platforms allow us to communicate with friends, work colleagues, groups, and strangers in the real world. They rely on person-to-person and person-to-group and person-to-world contact. We willingly post, and others look at, observe and comment on what we have to say, or share.

The metaverse is not that. The metaverse is likely to be all encompassing. It won't be a place where you post your status, it will *be* your status. It won't be a place where you share your latest real evening meal out, it will be the place where you enjoy your evening. Others will be able to join you, not just see pictures afterwards. We may experience no conscious difference between social media and the metaverse at all.

When this is considered, social media feels so - well, so linear. Comment, respond. Post, Like. Post, Like. Share, re-share.

What we have previously called sharing, we may recognize as actually 'broadcasting' in the hope of a response. The metaverse is likely to be far more experiential. In the metaverse, we may get closer to the idea of sharing, because we can literally share experiences at the same time.

We can join friends and colleagues in virtual worlds, or in metaverse experiences. We may well have virtual walls onto which we post ideas, pictures, and comments, just like on Facebook or LinkedIn, but why post a 'Like' when you can arrange to meet virtual friends in a park, to have a good old catch up almost in person?

It is very likely social media may continue to exist in

some form or another in the real world and be intimately connected with the metaverse. What you post on Facebook will appear in any virtual space you visit too. Any conversations you have over WhatsApp will continue in and out of the metaverse. And real world social media will reflect what you have been up to in the metaverse, whether in virtual reality or engaged in some other function such as exchanging currency or creating designs or presentations.

But in the metaverse, social media is likely to become fully integrated into our online lives. Instead of posting questions on a shop's Facebook or Instagram, and waiting for an answer, we'll be able to walk up to (or summon) an avatar from that shop, to put our questions directly (probably to an artificially intelligent responder).

Instead of posting a pretty flower arrangement on Pinterest, or a bird box for that matter, we'll simply bring it to a place in the virtual world and add it to a gallery that our virtual avatars can walk around.

Many of us will be members of Facebook groups, covering our interests, where we discuss, share images and gain knowledge. While these are likely to stay in place, we may see a converging of the virtual space and the flat-screen space, in metaverse groups. We can meet other members of those groups, in avatar form, to demonstrate how to fix a bike, or build a brick wall, or decorate our gardens; or to debate politics, discuss computer programming, share our writing, or showcase a latest presentation. We'll meet for yoga and Pilates sessions, join runs and cycle rides, or invite other members of the group for a game of virtual badminton.

And such behavior may become as natural to us as sitting on the bus posting about the exhibition we just visited. And if we thought social media was an immediate platform - post a Tweet, and you'll get responses right away - compare that to the metaverse, where we won't be posting our experiences, we'll be living them along with others.

In the same way, we might see dating Apps transfer in one way or another to virtual spaces, particularly because it reduces some of the emotional and physical risk that those seeking new friends and partners currently experience.

We might, for example, still swipe left or right for those we would like to meet, but algorithms could create virtual world coffee shops or bars in which everyone who's shown an initial interest in each other gets to meet in avatar form. The algorithm might create 'rooms' of people who have the same interests, or are looking for the same kinds of partner. Avatars will be able to chat, get to know each other, and decide whether to take a virtual table together, or whether to move on to another avatar. The emphasis on meeting one-to-one might be removed, instead of something more formal - for those who want it.

But once again, the metaverse may add value and difference to the dating experience. It might provide some of the experiences we would normally expect from a speed dating or speculative dating evening - short time limited chats, real views of people's faces and bodies, an idea of how a potential partner behaves in a particular situation. But it may also be augmented with additional useful information which might not be available, or even be purposefully hidden, by the person we're engaging with, in a real life situation: their marriage or partnership status, their criminal record perhaps, their resume even.

It would be for users of these experiences to decide what they'd want to see, and what users are willing to share about themselves. One could imagine a room full of people who have proven they are not married, for example. Or, indeed, a room full of people who are looking for something extra on the side of their marriage. All clearly declared upfront, with full awareness of participants and reduced risk for those who decide to enter.

This way, potential partners might meet for months in the metaverse before they actually decide to meet in person. Indeed, some might decide never to meet in person at all. And the metaverse may provide for their every need: from virtual date venues, like walks in wonderful parks or along river sides, to discreet virtual hotel rooms where they can securely share video conferencing, images, and even - with the development of sensory gloves and pressure pads - intimate touching.

We may giggle, but this is exactly what some people would prefer. For example, if they are just getting back into the dating game, or if for some other reason they are not able to access 'traditional' ways of meeting and dating people, perhaps because of mental or physical illness, crushing depression or exclusion, distance or even prison. Or if they have particular kinks, or preferences that are hard to match on a small scale, the metaverse might allow them to access a global community of likeminded souls.

Of course, there are abuse, privacy, control, consent, bullying, safety, and child safeguarding considerations to all of this, not just dating, but so does any kind of meeting over the internet and metaverse. All of that should be a priority as the metaverse develops, and is discussed in detail towards the end of this book.

Immersive experiences

One way to reframe the social media world into the metaverse is to look at what companies are planning to do as the future internet develops.

A great example is the willing creation of experiences for us all to enjoy, rather than something we have to watch, read, or listen to in a passive way. We may have all seen the Frozen movies, by Disney. Some of us may have met the 'Princesses' at one of the Disney theme parks. And we may well have posted about those fun experiences on our social media.

But none of us have actually interacted with the real characters, as we understand them from the films, because that interaction isn't possible with an animated film. We're real, they're cartoons. Right?

Until now.

According to the British Guardian newspaper, Disney's former executive vice-president of digital, Tilak Mandadi, wrote a LinkedIn post in 2020 about creating a Disney theme park metaverse, where the "physical and digital world converge" through wearable devices and mobile phones.

"Our efforts to date are merely a prologue to a time when we'll be able to connect the physical and digital worlds even more closely, allowing for storytelling without boundaries in our own Disney metaverse," he told shareholders.

Though no further plans have been announced, we can assume ideas such as interactive experiences are being considered at the very least. Perhaps interactive films where participants get to join in the adventures of Disney characters.

If we may let our imaginations run for a moment, we can think of an experience where we and our children get to meet Princesses Elsa and Anna, and speak to them in very accurate 3D form, within the virtual world. Those characters may have so many interactions with children and adults, that the artificial intelligence that 'powers' them, may learn the answers and responses to all questions and experiences, and be able to respond in an almost real way, and certainly convincing for kids. In a very experiential way, we will be meeting the *real* Elsa and Anna. Because surely they are as real in the virtual world as they are in digital format in a film?

From here, it doesn't take much to leap to, say, Marvel characters. Even though they're played by real actors in the films, much of the rest of the films are CGI created, including movements and expressions on the actor's faces. With more development, we may be able to meet the Hulk, or Nebula or Black Widow in the metaverse, and they may be able to respond in real time, their actions and responses purely driven by AI.

And don't forget how amalgamated the virtual and the real world will be. We will be able to 'touch' these characters with our sensory gloves. We will be able to create selfies of them and us, and then export them to the real world, by posting them on our Instagram accounts. We may even decide to have a 3D printer create a miniature but accurate 3D model of us, standing among the Avengers.

And these characters will not get tired. Their time will not be limited. They could have selfies with 1,000 kids at a time, and not one of those kids would know the difference. (The only people who might get tired are the lawyers attempting to protect copyright of Disney's characters and intellectual property.)

How does Santa Claus know what so many children in the world want for Christmas? The metaverse is your answer. If it is your tradition, you may well decide to visit Santa this year, at the North Pole, and spend some real time there with your kids, enjoying a long chat with the old man, stroking and feeding his reindeer, and playing with his elves.

In the Islamic tradition you may carry out the hajj, the pilgrimage to the holy city of Mecca in Saudi Arabia, in a next-to-real sense, even if you are unable to travel there. During Covid-19, the Saudi Hajj Ministry restricted the number of pilgrims to the site to a maximum of 10,000, rather than the 2.5 million they welcome ever year. In response, a German company created a virtual experience of visiting Mecca, called Muslim 3D.

Our very idea of what a 'real experience' is may well be disrupted in the development of the metaverse. We'll talk about meeting Elsa. We'll talk about going on the pilgrimage to Mecca. And we'll mean and understand it as having gone there, just as much as if we actually had.

If you doubt it, how many times have we said we've talked to someone, when actually we've had a WhatsApp conversation with them - leaving short messages for each other - over a longer period of time? It won't be long until we say: "I saw that band live" when what we mean is we attended a virtual concert.

And one more thing about augmented reality and immersive events is this: who's augmented reality we are using? Or will we get to choose?

For example, one might go on a virtual tour of the White House. That virtual tour could be delivered by one interpretation, saying capitalism and the USA represents the best and most successful form of democracy on the planet, and be filled with stories of the founding fathers, Abraham Lincoln and Benjamin Franklin.

Another virtual tour might cite the building as the vipers' nest of anti-Muslim oppressors of freedom, and list a history of wars waged against the Islamic world, the foundation for controversial interrogation techniques, and oppressive foreign policy.

Or, as tech journalist Casey Newton puts it in TheVerge: "... we're looking at the US Capitol building. And most of us might have an overlay that says, "This is the building where Congress works." And then some people might see an overlay that says, "On January 6, 2021, our glorious revolution began" [referring to the invasion of the US Capitol Hill by pro-Trump protestors]. And then maybe some other people see an overlay that says, "Lizard people are inside doing experiments on humans."[1]

Live events and gatherings

In December 21, two employees of virtual reality company eXp Realty, who had met at a virtual reality conference hosted by the company, held a real wedding in Florida and a virtual reality wedding that was streamed to employees who couldn't attend. The avatars the couple had created 'exactly matched' the wedding garments they wore, and a friend manipulated the movements of the avatars to mirror what was going on during the real life ceremony.[2]

This is a great example of how the metaverse may give a wider opportunity for everyone to share events in their lives, as well as join in events, gatherings, and gigs they might not otherwise be able to share.

While the couple's wedding didn't take place 'in' a virtual space, as such, the mirroring of it created a 3D experience that those who couldn't attend could experience, from various angles, and various distances. Something that's simply not possible with photographs or a wedding video.

This just touches on what may become general fare for experiences and gatherings in the metaverse.

"When two million people watch the exact same event together, not in one room or a slightly different synchronized version but the same exact version of that event, that is the closest you can get to, in my opinion, the definition of the metaverse,"

Jacob Navok, CEO of Genvid Technologies, who works in cloud computing was speaking to the Washington Post. He was referring to the tendency for artists, particularly pop artists, to host concerts online in Fortnite and other virtual spaces, during the Covid-19 pandemic.

Suddenly unable to allow people to gather in large crowds - the lifeblood of any artist's main income - some acts decided to go online to try out an alternative way to be seen and earn. With lots of success, not least Marshmello who drew ten million people onto Fortnite for a virtual concert in the game.

Duran Duran performed in Second Life in 2006. Phil Collins appeared in Grand Theft Auto performing his single In The Air Tonight. Travis Scott, BTS, Diplo, and Ariana Grande gave concerts in Fortnite as interactive experiences. Billie Eilish played at The Consumer Electronics Show in 2021, on a virtual platform called Spatial Web. Fortnite still offers smaller scale events on a regular basis.

Some promoters have gone further and organized full online, virtual festivals. In 2020, the world famous Glastonbury Festival cancelled its physical event because of Covid-19, but hosted an entirely online New Horizons festival, with four virtual music tents, over two days. It was

3D, but not virtual reality, so participants could join in via their computer screens. Fifty acts, including DJ Carl Cox, Fatboy Slim, and Alabama 3 performed on stage as either a 2D hologram, or a 3D custom avatar. Participants created avatars themselves, and could dance together in real time to the music.

"The outlandishness of the real world translates perfectly into VR," says a reviewer of the event from the VRScout YouTube channel. "It offers an opportunity for creators and players alike to take that absurdity even further with custom avatars and digital effects that would be impossible to replicate in real life."

At the Secret Sky 2021 festival, the acts may have been live or on screens, but the festival was entirely virtual. As one reviewer reported in the NME: "The virtual reality and browser-based event was an ode to the power of live music. The website teleported fans to a lush field full of robed avatars representing real people. Forgoing usernames, every attendee was simply marked with their physical location. White circles on the floor let players join voice chats and mingle with other groups from around the world. I danced in virtual reality with fans from Italy, ID'd tunes with a fast friend from Colombia and anticipated sets with users from the US and Japan over the course of the day."[3]

These virtual events may have been incredible, but they are not the same as real gigs. What many advocates of the metaverse have missed is that ten million people did *not* actually see the Marshmello event. The technology isn't strong enough yet. Actually, only 99 people shared that experience at any one time. The concert was actually just over 101 thousands of 99 people concerts, all run at the same time. Oh, and the concert was only ten minutes long.

So, when companies boast about what the metaverse

can do, we all need to retain some doubt, because the technology simply isn't there. But does that matter? Once again, if we expected the metaverse to give us a real experience of seeing our favorite bands in the flesh, surrounded by hot and sweaty other fans, singing along and as euphoric as we are, then perhaps we're asking too much.

Or more specifically, asking for the wrong thing.

While advocates of the metaverse have claimed we'll be able to join thousands, even millions, watching a band from all over the world, no-one has promised that it would actually feel like being at a concert with all those people.

Do we want to be at a concert with a million other people in real life? We'd never even see the act. We'd end up watching them on a huge screen. And that isn't a huge difference between watching them on a screen at home, or on YouTube.

It is worth repeating, the metaverse will not attempt to mirror real life. It will offer different experiences which we can take and enjoy for ourselves, not as substitutes for what we can do offline.

I may sure as hell like to attend a Foo Fighters' gig in real life, just about be able to see Dave Grohl and come home with my ears ringing, covered in bruises from bouncing up and down to Everlong. That's all good.

But I'd also like to experience that same concert in the metaverse, where I can stop to go for a pee without having to fight through the crowd, rewind to watch a song again, bring in a friend who couldn't attend the actual gig, and not have to take a shower afterwards.

Either way, I can get the merchandise, but in the virtual world there would be no queue to get my personally signed virtual T-shirt from Grohl himself.

Gaming

If sharing information and knowledge was the foundation of the internet, then gaming is surely the foundation of the metaverse. After all, hasn't playing a game on a screen always been a way of totally engaging ourselves into an alternative universe? Even if that universe is made up of well-known soccer or baseball players.

As the Economist website puts it: "Where the tech titans have money, the games industry has experience".

Step by step, our desire for information and sharing, and our desire for hands on entertainment, has brought the online world around so quickly, it sometimes feels like the latest hardware and software we use, or download, are already out of date by the time we unbox them.

The role of computer gaming in our online and virtual desires simply cannot be understated. We continuously want games to become more immersive, more realistic (even if the characters are dragons), more complex, more interactive, and we've wanted the ability to share playing those games with others we know, as well as with strangers.

Like evolution, gaming has responded to our ever changing desires, as well as our environments (faster speeds, better graphics), and it has also offered us opportunities and experiences we didn't know we wanted. Some were successful, like PlayStation and Xbox. Some were less so, like the gamut of handheld gaming options like PS4 Remote Play, the Wii U gamepad, and the iconic Gameboy, which were very quickly replaced by smartphones that did all the same things, and far more.

Established computer gaming platforms are already at the forefront of developing spaces which could already be regarded as metaverses, in which lots of the ingredients of the metaverse already exist: 3D virtual worlds, interactive socialization and gaming, shopping, trading in virtual currencies, building and creating, acting as platforms for advertising by online and offline brands. Many, such as Roblox, no longer define themselves as games platforms, but as social ones.

And commentators predict there will be a rapid surge in new gaming companies, looking to fill new spaces that the metaverse opens up. But, for those who aren't particularly interested in gaming (I include myself), let's look at today's main players that we're likely to hear a lot more from. This is because they will already bring a dedicated fanbase of players with them as the metaverse develops.

Fortnite - An online adventure game, launched in 2017, but which has grown into a number of different 3D games, with different abilities to build within real time action. During its Galacticus event, the game hosted 15 million players at once. Another 3.5 million watched the game on YouTube. Fortnite has toyed with initiatives that make it look more like a metaverse platform, such as hosting concerts and events, and taking sponsorship. In December 2019, CEO Tim Sweeney tweeted that Fortnite wasn't yet a metaverse platform, 'but ask me that question in a year's time.'

Minecraft - A 3D game, where players construct items and play games with simple 3D blocks. While the emphasis is on building worlds, there are games to be played, wars to be fought, and creators can build their own games and challenges within the game. The sheer number of players (over 130 million people played Minecraft once a month in 2020) and the ability to create within the game, makes Minecraft a key stakeholder in the emerging metaverse.

Roblox - No longer regarded as a gaming platform, but

more like a creative and sharing platform, Roblox allows players to create their own games and experiences, which other players can participate in, contribute to, and share. Like Fortnite, the platform has its own currency, which can be spent and earned.

Decentraland - Calls itself 'the virtual platform for digital assets'. Decentraland isn't owned by any single company, but rather by its users. Participants can build their own worlds within the platform, buying and selling land and goods, using two types of currency, protected by blockchains. Those who own the currency can vote on different issues within the platform, including its future development. Widely regarded as the most democratic of platforms, many will look at the model closely to avoid criticisms that one single company or group of companies are 'in control' of the metaverse.

Oculus - Meta's leading headset and games design platform offers a range of games from Facebook partners, and is the location of where Meta's development of the metaverses' virtual world is likely to take place. With the backing of Meta, Oculus is likely to further blur the distinction between gaming and the rest of the metaverse. A game from a Meta partner called Half-Life: Alyx is already well regarded as the most realistic picture of gaming in the metaverse, with its ultra-high rendering and its specific build for Oculus headsets.

Gaming as a living experience

As you can see from above, assessing what is a game, and what is a gaming platform, indeed what *was* a game and is *now* a platform, is complex. Gaming is continuing to evolve, and in the metaverse the border between gaming and not gaming at any one time might itself become blurred.

We have already covered 'gaming' military operations, and the potential for the metaverse to allow us to 'game' school and company virtual evacuations in the event of a shooting or fire. That's not too far from doing these things for fun, or what already takes place in some of the less palatable (for me) games such as Grand Theft Auto and other games that will be created by the newly empowered coders freely using the metaverse's creative platforms - all quite reasonably, and legally.

Even before the metaverse, we can see the merging between types of games. In the gaming world of yesterday, we might download a game - say a soccer game - and play it, among friends, or strangers, but safely and anonymously.

Today, we can play that same game, but there might be an element of payment and reward. We earn credits or currency for winning games or winning a league. We can use that to buy other players from other gamers to continue our winning spree. With good track records, and lots of gaming currency, we can join better higher up leagues.

Suddenly, instead of a game, our online soccer experience has become one of managing, bartering, accumulating income, dismissing players and - more likely than not - becoming personally and emotionally involved with the game.

Above, we have already discussed that gaming is a lifeline for even minimum earnings for kids in the Philippines. When money plays such a role, is computer gaming still a *game*, or an emotional and financial investment?

Let's translate those elements of playing virtual soccer into the metaverse. We may be able to market our kit, sell tickets to our games, get real Metacoin sponsorship from big brands to appear on banners in our stadiums, win leagues and cups, and gain Metacoin prizes, build our own brands, maybe even sell our brand to merchandisers of everything from virtual clothes to virtual lunch boxes. It has happened overnight to personalities on YouTube, who's whole thing is playing games to a live YouTube audience. One of the richest YouTubers is PewDiePie, whose net worth is estimated to be in the ballpark of $40 million, and most of his money is earned doing just that.

Pre-Covid-19, gaming competitions could fill stadiums in the real world, with players in branded clothing in the middle of the crowd like boxers in a boxing ring, and thousands of spectators cheering them on. In multiplayer games, dozens of gamers team together in real world stadia to battle other teams. Each of the teams would bring thousands of followers, just like any football or netball team. They cheer, they holler, they buy merchandise, and they buy tickets to physically be at the game. All this when they could have just watched it all on YouTube at home.

The metaverse might be able to recreate this atmosphere, where thousands, or even millions of gamers, can follow their favorites, and attend their live battles among other like-minded fans.

Like these super-gamers, many are making very generous income from their sole job of gaming. There are millions to be made through gaming competitions and tournaments, with not only prize money at stake, but lucrative sponsorship and rights exchanges taking place. According to Esports Earnings, a Danish player called Johan Sundstein has earned over $7 million playing a game called Dota 1, an online battle game. It makes him the highest earning gamer in the world. This is a growing industry, and the metaverse is likely to flatten and increase access to it.

This is not to say it is a bad thing. I'm merely pointing out that the barriers between gaming, virtual life and real life could become ever more blurred as the metaverse develops.

There are also opportunities in the metaverse for smaller companies, and even individuals, in designing games in this space. At the heart of what metaverse companies envisage is a creator economy. Programers will be encouraged to use the tools provided to them, or even open source code, to create new games, experiences, and adventures in the metaverse. They may be able to pay others - designers, marketeers, architects - to help build their games, and charge users to play, offering prizes for those who win. But they may also earn from sponsorship opportunities, such as hosting a product launch in their game or showing advertising banners, or having teams or individuals sponsored.

Free to play

Alternative models of earning will also be available. The Free to Play (f2p) model is huge in gaming: the gamer themselves doesn't pay, at least not to play the game. But their eyes on advertising, and their credit cards open for merchandise, makes the model profitable. According to metaverse and gaming expert Jon Radoff, the f2p model accounts for 75% of revenue in the gaming industry in 2021, and by 2025 (presumably with the metaverse in its very early stages) is estimated to rise to 95%.

It is probably this motivation to earn from creating and building the metaverse that will keep the momentum of the metaverse going, rather than simply people's own motivation to create something new. If it relied only on motivation, one could suspect a virtual and online world full of not-quite-finished and abandoned games, stadiums, pitches, doorways leading to nowhere. The equivalent of millions of '404 not known' notifications we see when our internet browsers hit a dead page.

The future of gaming

But apart from income earning, what other opportunities for gaming will the metaverse offer that we don't currently experience? As always, there's the question of the unknown and unpredictable: gaming may move in ways none of us expect. But we can at least imagine.

For example, it is very likely that the role of artificial intelligence will play a bigger role. At a basic level, the AI of an adventure game you're playing in will 'learn' the moves you most often make, the strategies you use, the players, and weaponry, you prefer and why. It may then create new scenarios in which to play: those that are more fun, more challenging, easier, or harder, depending on what you requested. If you like fighting dragons, you'll find more dragons to fight against. While your friend, on their game, may find themselves fighting warlocks.

In the same way, algorithms may learn from how other players enjoy their games, what they build, what they want from their game play, and the games may test those out with you. Any advertising in the games you play may learn what you respond to and what you don't, delivering only adverts that tend to get you to click.

In an ever increasing and more detailed learning loop,

each game may wrap around its players over weeks and months of playing, creating very unique experiences and game play that cannot be compared with others. You may begin playing a monster based battle game at the beginning of the month, but in 30 days' time you might be fighting vampires, because those monsters have evolved into vampires in response to the kind of weapons (silver crosses, wooden stakes) that you prefer to use, or the kinds of playing lands you choose to join.

Another example, not difficult to imagine. Many have considered the touch, sight, and hearing sensations in the metaverse, but little has been said of taste and smell. As Aaron Mak writes on the satirical website Slate: "If Facebook was asking us to imagine the mind-bending experiences that the metaverse makes possible, a party for scented candles where you can't actually smell the candles would seem to fall short."

But it's not too far a leap to imagine that those senses may be integrated into our gaming experience too. Considering the prevalence of brands like Red Bull, Coca Cola, Gatorade, Subway, crisp and chips brands in the sporting world, including current online games like FIFA and F1 racing. The virtual universe may open up an opportunity for brands to enrich gaming experiences by, for example, delivering packets of scents, or samples to taste, to those who download a particular game so they cement the brand and the taste while playing. Gamers love to snack. Imagine if Doritos had a virtual stall at the side of a soccer pitch, allowing you to order free samples, which might be delivered the same or next day.

Or, if we stretch our imagination even further, we might not be too far away from the world of sensory implants. Along with our VR headsets, we could posit a metaverse where, with a small attachment above the ear, our brains could be tricked into believing we could smell, or taste, a particular product during gaming. Or anywhere else in the metaverse for that matter, like a perfume or chocolate shop.

Or in a more crude sense, there might be canisters of a mix of smells and tastes, that could release different proportions of each into the air, to recreate the sensation of smelling a Subway shop. It's long been suspected that coffee shops, bakeries, and big chains release smells into the shopping experience to do just that. Why not in the metaverse? We could link the virtual drinking of a can of cola with the sensation of tasting, smelling, and swallowing it.

If there are extra sales to be made from the development of such technology, there's no reason to imagine some entrepreneurs aren't already on the job. Indeed, the University of Chicago have developed a way to get people to feel hot and cold in virtual reality with smells, by manipulating the trigeminal nerve in the nose, which carries sensory information like smell and temperature between the brain and the face. Tubes extending to the users' nose send puffs of the chemicals every six seconds. The hardware is impractical just now, but like everything may become smaller, cheaper, and perhaps more effective as time goes by.

Perhaps most significant, when it comes to gaming in the metaverse, will be the interchangeability within games and what the rest of the metaverse offers. Gamers will no longer be confined to the games they're playing in. In fact, the games are likely to be part of the metaverse, not separate from it.

And we will move between games, shops, experiences, and adventures seamlessly. Imagine creating a funky skin in

Fortnite, then taking it to FIFA and playing a game of football with your team while wearing it. You win the cup, and take it to Second Life and sell it for Metacoin. That gives you enough currency to buy a ready-made new house in Minecraft, as well as a car in a Roblox racing game.

Once again, we have no reason to imagine the virtual world of the metaverse will mirror our own real world. There will be no up or down, nor right or left, nor limit in the distance or behind us.

Doors can lead to new lands, Narnia like, even though there are virtual walls behind them. We can leap from where we are standing at any one time, into places far away, or even in a different virtual dimension. We will as readily choose the games we play by selecting them from a wall of options, as we may walk down a virtual street or visit a virtual theme park. Stadiums will never get full. The number of players in a game could be unlimited.

The metaverse offers the future of gaming, but not as we know it. We probably won't even call it gaming any more.

Take aways

- The metaverse is likely to grow out of social media, may replace it or at least envelop it.
- Interacting with others in the metaverse may become as natural to us as checking our emails or searching on Google.
- We may be able to have fully immersive experiences, such as interacting with cartoon characters and visiting museums.
- Games companies are likely to be seeking new

opportunities in the metaverse, turning their games into fully interactive platforms.

- Gaming will become a live experience for those gaming, and those watching games who will gather in virtual places to watch.

GOVERNANCE AND DEMOCRACY

The Washington Post had one of the real challenges of the metaverse pinned down, when it published a speculative article in April 2020, by Gene Park. The journalist wrote about the launch of a new social platform called Quibi, and how it showcased film watching within the platform by re-running a series that had first run in Fortnite. Some users were more pleased than others.

"As players logged on to watch the show inside the game, other players started to build their forts to block the screen. Any openings left were pelted by tomatoes. It was a stark reminder that even though the Metaverse may evolve from the internet, the way we behave on it may not be so easily changed."[1]

The metaverse is likely to be one of the most interesting and exciting things to happen to the social internet for a very long time, and it's easy to get carried away with the opportunities that it is going to provide. But the key question remains: who's in charge? Who gets to stop (or encourage) tomato pelting of other user's experiences?

Does the metaverse need an internal government, and if

so, what does this look like? Might the metaverse generate its own government? Its own elections, which govern what's allowed and what's not? And what happens when that internal government conflicts with users, or perhaps more significantly, with the companies that run the metaverse, or real life governments? What about if artificial intelligence plays a role in the internal government of the metaverse? And how far must the internal government of the metaverse coincide, or be instructed, by real world government and democracy.

These may seem like philosophical questions, but they're ones that will need to be asked more and more as the metaverse develops. Because in turn they generate further questions about ownership, governance of the new social space, privacy, child and vulnerable adult protection, copyright protection, the potential dangers of AI, and of addiction.

Metaverse expert and commentator Matthew Ball writes: "the metaverse will need altogether new rules for censorship, control of communications, regulatory enforcement, tax reporting, the prevention of online radicalization, and many more challenges that we're still struggling with today."

Some may envisage these things will 'find their place' as the metaverse emerges proper. After all, how can we predict and perhaps legislate for something that has not happened yet? Others are more circumspect, looking back at how the internet has developed and how governments and companies alike seem to be constantly outrun by issues on social media platforms like bullying, anti-vaccine messages, fake news, freedom of speech, the dark web, hacking, incitement to hatred, porn, and addiction. Authorities have been left to rely on the goodwill, or the threat of legislation, for social media companies to do more to deal with these kinds of postings on their platforms.

On top of that are simply the questions of how the internet of the past - where companies have worked mainly in silos, owning their own platform, refusing to share code, hardware, programming protocols, even floor space - can simply flip that model into something based on sharing.

We cannot kid ourselves that the profitable business model of obtaining a customer and keeping them - iPhone or Samsung? PlayStation or Xbox? Mac or PC? Safari, Chrome, Firefox, or Explorer? - will be broken down into a sharing paradise. Facebook can decide, or not, to remove content. Amazon can choose to display a book, or not. What if these platforms disagree in the metaverse about what should be seen?

Throughout the researching and writing of this book, I've read and heard statements that a particular company is already creating its own version of the metaverse: Fortnite, Meta, Minecraft, and Decentraland all fall into this category. Which begs the question: if they're all doing that already using their own coding and protocols, then some people's vision of a united seamless metaverse is unrealistic?

Some commentators accused Meta (previously Facebook) of lumping into the metaverse space with its money, brand, and power, almost claiming it was its own invention, when other companies had already been developing virtual worlds, currencies, and augmented realities for years.

In his interview with TheVerge, Mark Zuckerberg seemed to go half-way towards the sharing model, but also hinted at Meta-only owned property too, illustrating perhaps some of the heavy creases that will need to be ironed out.

The announcement that Meta is going to recruit 10,000 new coding staff in Europe surely can't be based on creating something that all the other companies will enjoy a healthy profit from.

The company isn't known for doing things that doesn't bring more money into its own accounts. The company already has more than 10,000 people working on augmented and virtual reality projects in its Reality Labs division. It has already bought up other artificial reality companies - BigBox VR, Unit 2 Games, Beat Games, Sanzaru Games and Ready at Dawn - in contrast, perhaps, to its stated aim of widening the opportunities for individual creators and developers in the metaverse.

He tells TheVerge: "So for our part, for example, we're building out the Quest headsets for VR, we're working on AR headsets. But the software that we build, for people to work in or hang out in and build these different worlds, that's going to go across anything. So other companies build out VR or AR platforms, our software will be everywhere. Just like Facebook or Instagram is today. So I think part of this is, I think it'll be good if companies build stuff that can work together and go across lines rather than just being locked into a specific platform."

By its very nature, the metaverse is going to encourage these challenges, and as Matthew Ball suggests, some of them will need to be fixed before users (and governments) trust it, and others will be fixed as it is developed. The danger is that excitement about the technology once again runs away from our ability to manage and govern it.

It is worth revisiting some of the principles of the envisaged metaverse that will come into play here.

Interoperability

This is the idea that different parts of the metaverse will work together, so that users have a seamless experience. They may be able to listen to music on Spotify, while wearing clothes they'd designed in Fortnite and shopping on Amazon in a virtual world, and the goods will be delivered to their address in the real world.

For this to happen, platforms will have to share their deepest codes with each other. Currently it is possible to share certain logins for programs online: you may have been asked to create a new login for an App, or been given the option to login using your Google or Facebook account. That's a very basic level of sharing.

The metaverse will need to go much deeper. It will require almost total integration of data, so that avatars (with all their data, currency, property etc.) can move between games, shopping, platforms, and more.

First, comes the question of how far platforms will be willing to share that data with each other, given that the whole value of their business model is surely exclusive ownership of their users' data and information. Without exclusive access to our searching patterns on Google, for example, how can Google maintain itself as an advertising sales venue that ultra-targets its users?

Second, will be the question of whether we, as users, allow platforms to share our data in this way. We may decide to share our personal data with Amazon, but prefer to share the bare minimum with Facebook, eBay, TikTok, or whatever new and controversial online platform is invented.

If the metaverse doesn't offer us the choice about who gets our data, then perhaps we won't engage in it. Or more likely, the companies will see our desire to protect our data and put their interests above the wider metaverse, creating exactly the silos the metaverse is supposed to overcome.

Finally, the technical progress and sheer coder hours required for the true integration of platforms should not be underestimated. It is not like these programs already have ready-to-open pipes between them, and the tap just needs to be turned on so that they can work together. Acres and acres of computer programming and digital database integration will be needed to make even the simplest of sharing possible.

Raph Koster, multiplayer online gaming expert, has recently written a series of blog articles about how 3D designing 'game objects' (such as food, or a sword, or a skin) works.

"We should not underestimate the magnitude of the task of figuring out what value a cooked pie from Breath of the Wild has in Halo - or mapping every game to every other game," he says. "There are no standards right now for 'what things can do' in a virtual world, and we shouldn't want them. The act of setting the standard is also setting the limit, which would curb creativity enormously. There's far too much possibility to be explored still".

"If you can carry food to a new world and eating restores health, that might really unbalance a game where you aren't supposed to be able to heal at all".[2]

Not only that, but designing and playing games - or shopping, or building new exciting things, or ordering online - won't be such fun if everything runs in exactly the same way all the time. Surely, part of a game is discovering that if you eat the green fruit, you get taller, and if you eat the red one, you get shorter. But apply that across all games, indeed, across the whole 'integrated' metaverse platform, and it becomes rather 'meh!'

Wes Fenlon at PC Gamer magazine, who cites Koster's article, goes on to ask in his must-read article *The metaverse is bullshit*: "Does every metaverse-compatible game just become a mushy Fortnite glob of everything mixed together?"

Not only this, but there is the question of contradictory experiences in the metaverse. In his launch video for Meta, Mark Zuckerberg unwittingly illustrates the problem.

In the gaming section of his launch video, Zuckerberg in full VR avatar form stands as he watches a game of virtual table tennis, then is invited by a friend to 'port in', to come 'down for a VR foiling sesh', which turns out to be virtual reality surfing - like in the sea. He surfs the virtual waves with his buddy (without getting wet), with water tumbling over his head and crashing into boats. But then in another section of the same video, he meets some friends playing poker in zero gravity, and floats around the virtual room with them. So, which is it Mr Zuckerberg - gravity or no gravity in the VR parts of the metaverse? Because surely you can't have both, or at least not if you want platforms to interact, some of which don't have gravity in their games, with others that do?

If platforms are to become integrated, who makes the rules? Gravity or no gravity? 'Death' of a character after three strikes, or an endless gaming life? Can I murder someone in the metaverse? Can I stand in exactly the same place as someone else in the 3D world, or is there a social distance for the sake of a 'real computer generated experience'?

The crux is this: if coders are already keenly programming new codes for virtual worlds and new experiences around and about the metaverse, is there an equally hard working and keen set of coders creating protocols and standards so that different platforms can fit their experiences together? And who gets to decide what rolls and what doesn't?

When simple sharing of information online grew out of Tim Berners-Lee's technology lab and eventually became the internet, it was necessary to create a set of protocols so that information could be presented in an easy-to-read and understand way. This is what HTML became. It stands for Hypertext Markup Language.

Across the internet, whoever or whatever is designing the pages you see can use HTML in one version or another to ensure what they intend to show as **bold**, appears that way in your internet browser. And when they want something to appear underlined, they use HTML to tell the browser that's what should happen.

After HTML, a complimentary web design language was established called CSS. The Cascading Style Sheet would allow graphical flourishes to web pages, making text and images even more pleasant to look at, and more adaptable to being viewed in different web browsers.

Neither the metaverse, nor virtual reality, nor augmented reality, nor even 3D experiences on a 2D screen, have a set of standard protocols, or anything like it. Each does its own thing.

That's why even in 2021, my son can't play FIFA 21 on his PlayStation against someone playing the same FIFA 21 game on their Xbox.

If that's a challenge to the big companies, their vision of opening the metaverse up to smaller entrepreneurs in a shared creative economy, looks insurmountable just now.

Sharing and open code

Another vision for the metaverse, as already described, is the principle of open code. In short, it is envisaged there will be at least three levels of coding in the metaverse. Raw code, which expert computer programmers will be able to use to create something from basically nothing, with codes that you and I could not possibly understand. Secondly, there will be a series of coding platforms where users will be able to create games, functions, shapes, and more using existing pre-programmed coding blocks which they drop into place to build something new. Thirdly, there will be user-ready platforms where those with no experience of building computer games, programs, or online presences, can simply plug-and-play into a platform to choose between various options, such as colors, shapes, pre-written instructions, to create something new. There are likely to be lots of levels between these, but the principle is the same.

I've already written about the benefits of this shared protocol, and touched on some of the difficulties of it when different companies will have their own 'blocks' of codes, that may not interact well with each other. If I build something in Minecraft right now - a classic example of the third level of creation - I would not be able to export that item or building into Fortnite, or into a more general metaverse space. The programming language simply isn't the same.

But this wider access to creation, design and sharing the metaverse comes with some other very serious implications. I will use extremes to demonstrate the point. In a shared metaverse, built eventually on shared programming lines, might not I be able to create in a particular platform - say in Roblox - a fully armored tank? Could I not then drive that tank 'out' of Roblox and into a virtual shopping mall, laying waste to other people's delicately created exhibitions, shops, even avatars?

If I can create a super-hero avatar, or even an evil avatar, in a game like Fortnite, could I not simply walk around other spaces in the metaverse in that same persona, deciding which other avatars I'm seeing are criminals, or people I don't like the look of, and simply take them down?

Ah, the creators of the metaverse might say, we'll have protocols - rules - that prevent that. But if the code is truly open, could an expert coder not easily create something that circumvents any rules, because that is the point of open-code? If I can see the open-code, then surely I can program around it, or design an avatar or object that does not abide by that code. Meta introduces gravity. My avatar is programed to ignore that?

And let's say someone 'evil' has destroyed my brand new metaverse building in their Roblox tank, could I not just push a button, and have it all immediately recreated at no cost to me? Would that kind of insurance cost money, or will it be hard coded into the platform? And if so, what value is a crypto currency, if a non-fungible asset can simply be recreated at the touch of a button.

I write these extreme ideas to highlight how the programming of the metaverse doesn't only have to ensure that platforms can communicate with each other, and that new entrepreneurial entrants to the market can participate. Each of the participants will somehow need a governance structure.

And if the metaverse requires a governance structure, then it can't be a truly open-code system. *Someone or something* needs to be able to make decisions about what's allowed (investing in someone else's property) and what's not (using a tank to destroy someone else's property), and what's possible (pressing a button to rebuild your property in an instant).

And if that *someone or something* exists, who gets to choose it? Is there an election? A metaverse democracy? And if so, how is that governed across the world which have democracies of various different types and strengths?

For the metaverse to work for its users and the retail companies that invest in it, it needs to be stable and consistent. The more 'open' the platforms are, the more vulnerable they are likely to be for instability and inconsistency. And these vulnerabilities will not only lead to distrust, but could lead to unpalatable outcomes such as a 'dark metaverse' which is totally ungoverned, not unlike the dark web, as well as unlimited fake news, harassment, hate speech, and more.

The illustration is clear: we have not been able to control or govern many of the worst areas of the internet we currently have, with governments and companies continuously passing the responsibility back and forward between each other. In the meantime, it is children, vulnerable adults, older people, and even everyday internet users that can be drawn into opinions, ideas, images, and other spaces they have no desire to be drawn into. Before we plough ahead into something new, should there not be space for solving the problems with shared networks that we already have?

My own novel *Portico*, deals in detail with this issue of freedom of speech and governance of social media.

Fake 'news' and harmful content

A key principle of the metaverse is its integration with the real world, through augmented and virtual reality but also in the way we use the metaverse in our daily real lives. From accessing news and opinions, to spending our money and leisure time.

In our lives right now, we are vulnerable to being fed fake news and content that we shouldn't or don't want to see. My own children have admitted to faking their date of birth, so they can play on Fortnite (minimum age 13). The violent game Grand Theft Auto has a minimum player age of 17 in the USA, and 18 in the rest of the world. In a fully integrated metaverse, if our kids can subscribe (or indeed we allow them) to access Grand Theft Auto, will that not open them to everything else that is only acceptable for over 18s? That assumes a shared protocol of age restriction, and faces all the problems mentioned above: Who gets to decide? How can this be validated? In open source, can't it just be circumvented?

The challenge of harmful content on the internet today does not restrict itself only to those who have declared themselves as over 18 anyway, or in Facebook's case 13. Any child is just a few clicks away from seeing content that is not appropriate for them, whether that be porn, extremist videos, self-harm, or bootlegged videos of films they wouldn't otherwise be able to see.

And it's not just about our kids or vulnerable adults. Social media companies rely on us creating echo chambers around ourselves. Their algorithms depend on it, and gladly assist it. I rarely see ideas I disagree with popping up on my Facebook feed. The advertising and feeds that come my way are about cycling, writing, parenting, the environment.

Social media is designed that way, and it keeps me coming back.

If social media fed me advertising and posts I found distasteful or offensive, I wouldn't visit the platform quite so much, and they would lose all those vital clicks. Thus, we all create and then continue, with the help of internet platforms, our own bubbles that please us.

While that enables some of us to live in comfortable worlds of information about baking our own bread, helping the homeless, and supporting the health service, other's worlds are more comfortable if they receive information about how asylum seekers are bleeding our economy dry, how certain races or religions are inferior, or how particular unconventional cures are the answer to Covid-19. One person's harmful content or biased view is another's freedom of speech.

One government's idea of extreme content might not be the same as a social media company. And they may lay responsibility for it on each other.

Now imagine the same rolled out in the metaverse, which as we've already established is being pursued at breakneck speed, and far faster than governments can keep up with. Possibly more rapidly than the companies themselves can consider the harm implications for. Add to that the idea that it will be an open source space, where 'creators' might not always have a bright, rainbow lit, perfect sharing metaverse world in mind, but something entirely different.

It might seem like nit-picking, but online bullying, abuse, the dark web, online extremism, and hate speech are already widespread problems with the tools that we already have. Neither the main players in the space, nor governments, have been able to get on top of it. Why should we assume it's going to be any better in the metaverse? Particularly when governments can be so slow, and social media companies can be so resistant, leaning heavily on the crutch of freedom of speech (and their advertising revenue).

"As we continue to grapple with governance imperatives for artificial intelligence, the emergence and acceleration of augmented and virtual reality... presents a related and important governance frontier – raising novel and complex challenges for which we, and our legal system, are ill-prepared," according to Karen Silverman, Founder and Chief Executive Officer, The Cantellus Group and Thomas A. Campbell, Founder and CEO, FutureGrasp writing for the World Economic Forum. "The US relies heavily on litigation to establish functional boundaries on behaviors, resolve disputes, and interpret laws. This means that new enforceable standards take a long time to develop; tend to trail the emergence of societal norms and expectations; and tend to focus on edge cases that are decided by judges and juries with differing levels of expertise in this technology. It's also worth noting that in the US alone, more than 85,000 local government districts enforce laws governing everyday and extraordinary conduct – with many differences one to the next."

By its nature, legal process is slow. National and local government is slow. The internet is fast. The metaverse will be fast.

Only in August 21, did the White House Office of Science and Technology Policy begin exploring the possibility for a new Bill of Rights governing artificial intelligence: things like facial recognition, biometrics, voice analyzers, and other automatic processes. There's a whole consultation process to go through, ongoing as I write in early 2022. By the time anything is decided, presuming it passes, it will be out of date in regard to AI, let alone how AI is used in the metaverse.

It is another example of technology moving far quicker than any legislative process can keep up with. And perhaps those behind the metaverse like it that way.

As Kevin Roose from the New York Times pointed out the day after Meta was renamed, and Mark Zuckerberg's hopes for the future of the metaverse began to circulate: "One group that conspicuously wasn't pictured hanging out in the metaverse during Thursday's presentation? Politicians."[3]

Democracy and the metaverse

Tim Sweeny, CEO of Epic Games, which owns Fortnite writes: "This metaverse is going to be far more pervasive and powerful than anything else. If one central company gains control of this, they will become more powerful than any government and be a god on earth."

This from the head of one of the key platforms involved in the building of the metaverse. If he's worried, the rest of us should be too.

Matthew Ball signals a similar warning: "We're talking about a future state in which a company owns not just the devices we use, not just the payment services we use to purchase digital services, but the physics of our virtual world, the integration into our physical world. It is not government, it is not public research institutions, it is not independent consortiums of techno philosophers, who are driving the emergence of the metaverse, it is the wealthy and most powerful for-profit corporations on earth."

And as Micaela Mantegna writes in her research paper on the metaverse and its governance: "Governance challenges arise in similar ways to those already existing around the internet, only to be enhanced by the invasive and intimate nature of this immersive technology with sensors and devices connected close to the body and extracting biometric data - like eye tracking devices - that is ripe for abuse."[4]

Quite apart from democracy within the metaverse, and how the platforms police themselves, is the question of who is managing, policing, and setting boundaries for what those companies with an interest are allowed or not allowed to do. And what consequences they should face if they don't play along.

Perhaps we would look to our democratically governed leaders - and in many cases opposing parties, scrutinizing mechanisms and the media - to keep any eye on the unparalleled growth and power of the emerging metaverse.

But things are not as simple as that.

Social media has been widely credited, and also condemned, for interfering with political messages and, in extremes, 'winning' and 'losing' elections. Though sound research has found posting on social media has some influence in certain circumstances - Twitter was found to be a big draw to the liberal minded first voters in the 2020 US election, but it was also found to be generally friendly towards Donald Trump because he was seen as more 'real' - it has been difficult to match electoral wins with social media influence.

More concerning was the UK's campaign to either stay or leave its membership of the European Union, and the 2000 US election. Accusations flew in every direction about fake news, fake social media accounts, manipulation of video and images to make candidates look like they were making mistakes, or simply creating memes and other addictive easy-to-share posts that while not based in truth, were funny or poignant, and that were enough to give candidates a few more votes.

And these 'extras' on social media didn't have to be approved or sanctioned by the candidates or points of view they represented. They circulated apart from the mainstream campaigns, making it easy for the leaders of those campaigns to distance themselves from them.

"In the past few weeks leading up to Election Day, there has been a unique rise in cases of video manipulation where video clips are edited to make candidates appear to be making mis-steps that they didn't commit, slurring words or appearing less competent, and some deep fakes, a technique using artificial intelligence to fabricate images and videos most often used for malicious purposes, where videos are computer generated to show false footage," says a blog from the Division of Research and the University Maryland. It quotes Dr. Jen Golbeck, professor at the University in Information Studies (UMD iSchool) and expert in social networks.

"While [social media] platforms prohibit this, they often get posted, viewed, and shared millions of times," Golbeck said. "One of the main manipulation techniques used to add legitimacy to candidates and positions is to use bots or super active accounts to make things look popular."[5]

Golbeck identifies in her article some of the key ingredients that may have played a controversial role in the 2020 election in the US. Once again, apply these ideas to the metaverse of the future: artificial intelligence creating accounts, video (and VR) manipulation, fake news, an open creation space where individuals can create echo chambers, or public spaces that look real, but are influenced by a particular point of view or political persuasion.

Freedom of speech

If we can create an avatar of our choosing, why not one that looks exactly like the US President, or the UK Prime Minister, or the German Chancellor, and make them say incredible, even offensive things? Sure, we could ask for the metaverse companies to ban this, or monitor their platforms to remove these fake avatars, but how far will that betray their declared independence from politics?

And how far will it compromise freedom of speech? If I'm not allowed to make my avatar look like the President, am I allowed to make it look like, say, my local mayor? Or a pop star? Or my neighbor? Who gets to decide, and who gets to judge the amount of 'likeness' my image is allowed close to a real personality? Does that not take away the powerful tool of satire and our freedom to challenge our leaders through comedy?

It is tricky territory. Imagine sneaker and sports brand Nike releasing products into the metaverse, to be used by other companies as well as by individuals. A high profile individual, say a social media influencer, might buy a pair of unique designed Nike sneakers to wear in the metaverse. A lot of fuss ensures about the shoes, about the influencer and, of course, about Nike. All good things.

But what if that influencer, and their avatar, begins to post anti-Semitic language on their feeds? Can Nike *remove* that pair of sneakers that the influencer bought with their own Metacoin? And if they do, to whom does the influencer appeal and ask for their money back? What about freedom of speech? Or will Nike include with the sale a contract that says anyone who wears their sneakers must adhere to certain online rules?

Another example. How will boycotts work in the

metaverse? What if Israeli retailers, or even the Israeli government, wants to ban opportunities and virtual objects from being available to those who declare themselves to be supportive of the Palestinian government in the Gaza strip? Or even Hamas, which is regarded in most countries to be a terrorist group, but certainly not across much of the Arabic world. Will that be allowed? What if relationships between real nations break down, and governments want to cease real-life trading between the two countries, and want that to extend to the metaverse too?

Suddenly democracy doesn't look so sound in the metaverse. It leaves users disenfranchised. After all, who should we trust: the metaverse platforms who want us to share, share, share? The news and information which is appearing in the metaverse, which may or may not be true? The government actors who may want to restrict the metaverse and freedom of speech, but who might also be manipulating the platforms to their own ends?

As individuals and users of the metaverse, we might like to have an idea that we, ultimately, will be in control of such things. After all, can't we just walk away if we're not happy with how the metaverse is working out? But as everything from shopping to applying for government benefits, filing taxes to getting school and college places, moves into a new virtual internet, excluding ourselves may sound easier than it really is.

Skewed advertising

Note too the strong power of advertising. In the metaverse, just as in real life, we may be bombarded with persuasive advertising wherever we go, and wherever we look. Those adverts may be tailored to our own personalities, habits, desires, politics and, for example, where we stand on the Arab-Israeli conflict.

And in the same way, we may be prevented from seeking advertising and information that others hold, because it is not in their interest to share it with us. A quick look at the Facebook advertising platform makes this clear. If I'm setting up an advert I want a specific audience to see - say, people who support breast feeding until one year after birth - I can decide to target women of about 24 to 35 years old, who have shown an interest in breast feeding. I can also specifically *exclude* from my advertising others who I believe are not going to want to see my message, or I know won't agree with what I have to say. In Facebook advertising I can ensure that my advert is *not* shared with older women, with men, with people who've shown interest in particular faiths, or people who support particular charities.

In the metaverse, it means that information users might benefit from might not be available. I might have grown up in a religiously conservative family, and suddenly need advice about the termination of a pregnancy. That information might not be advertised to me, because my profile and my background says I'm less likely to want that product or information. Instead of information being available at side-of-the-road billboards or at bus stops, where one can see them and take down a web address or phone number privately, that information might be screened out for us because we are not a target audience.

Meantime, my metaverse world might automatically be filled with advertising that is anti-family planning, abortion, contraception, because my background and my profile says I'll be most responsive to those messages. All of this currently takes place on today's online platforms. The key point is that in the metaverse, where advocates say we might be spending up to 80% of our time each day, those adverts and messages are going to be all pervasive.

We may think we are in charge. We might be surprised.

Cyber attacks

The sheer value of the metaverse, even though it doesn't properly exist yet, means it may offer rich pickings for hackers and those who seek to exploit the new world and tools for their own gain - or simply for fun.

First, there is lots of money to be made, or stolen, from users in the metaverse who may not understand how money works in the new virtual space. It may be easy to fool users into giving up their currency or exchanging it for things that have no value.

Just as five year old kids don't understand that when they spend silver coins on our iPhone Apps, they're actually spending real money that will come out of Mom's account, even those of us who are older will look at the metaverse and wonder: how does this thing work? We may lose a lot of real money to scammers while we're trying to figure it out. That's not hacking, but it's in the same ballpark.

Second, there may be hackers who exploit the early weaknesses in the metaverse, and in blockchain managed currencies, to extract virtual and real money from its platforms using their pure coding skill, or AI they design to seek out weak code and bugs.

Third, hackers may exploit the junctures between platforms that meld together to make up the metaverse. There may be, for example, 'locations' where Metacoin of one type needs to be 'exchanged' for another type, along with relevant 'currency exchange rates'. On platforms that act super-fast, it will be possible to write codes that continuously exchange and lend currencies between platforms, earning just a little at a time from each transaction, but in the end - in a matter of minutes - exploiting inconsistencies sufficiently to earn a lot of money, and take it out of the metaverse economy.

Fourth, hackers might be able to 'kidnap' our avatars, assume our identities in the metaverse, and go on spending sprees, for their own personal gain. Once again, the nature of the metaverse is that a hijacked avatar - with the right hacker-created coding - will be able to carry out hundreds, or even thousands of transactions in the space of minutes. Well before we realize we've been hacked, or the 'governance' (whatever that looks like) of the metaverse steps in to stop it.

By which time our anonymous hacker, who could be our neighbor or a kid in Korea, just emptied our meta account - or even got access to our real life accounts too.

These incidents may be more difficult to "identify, verify, and bring under control, and it might be hard to ascertain where responsibilities lie in respect of breach notification to users and data protection authorities," according to legal experts.[6]

Why will the metaverse be so open to such cyberattacks?

Because it is new and exciting for hackers. Because early coding and the development of platforms, particularly in the exchanging of data between platforms, is likely to be full of glitches that can easily be exploited. Because of the declared desire by key players that the metaverse will be run using open source coding, to better enable creatives to make an entry into the platform. And because, for someone who hasn't got any money and wants some, learning to hack a fast developing world which is bound to be full of coding gaps, because companies are so keen to get there first, sounds a lot better than no money at all, or sweeping the streets for spare change.

It is not that internet companies and social media leaders aren't aware of hacking as a problem. All have experienced it.

During 2020, Facebook, Zoom, Microsoft, Nintendo, Twitter, and Whisper were all hacked, exposing millions of data records and information. Millions of pages of publicly censored data were released by international non-profit Reporters Without Borders within the Minecraft gaming platform.

All of the major players are planning for a world where hacking is a large risk in the metaverse, and smaller designers and creators will be urged to use particular tools too - just as our own devices continually tell us to upgrade our virus software.

The problem is that the metaverse is developing at pace, and no-one wants to wait for fully, absolutely secure channels to be built and tested before opening them up. The internet didn't evolve that way. If the technological world tried to design a metaverse in a box that had to be tested to its limits, that each platform agreed to, it would not only be far from what the user has been promised, it probably wouldn't happen at all.

As already discussed, these kinds of developments are evolutionary. In a sense, the metaverse needs to welcome the hackers and their methods, so that they can be tackled. And with each new development in the metaverse, new hacking techniques will be developed too, in a never ending chase that hopefully improves security over time.

But another challenge will be the ultra-global nature of the metaverse, and the sheer number of invested players and creators across the world. Finding security standards between so many agents is likely to be impossible, particularly as the metaverse continues to evolve and change, and new problems are highlighted.

As per the internet, it was impossible to plan for hate speech, offensive material, illegal porn, and extremist views and planning, before the internet emerged. We had to wait until those things emerged, before starting to tackle them. Even now, governments, companies and internet users have not concluded who is responsible for such content and who should be removing it, nor what is acceptable and what is not.

In a metaverse that is rapidly developing, and is open source so it has thousands and thousands of creators involved, the design and delivery of its elements will far outpace any governance or agreement about even technical standards. Hoping that the metaverse players will also be able to agree on standards and responsibility for tackling hacking, as well as hate speech or illegal porn, might be too much to ask.

Indeed, in a fully integrated metaverse, that allows freedom of creation, virtual and augmented reality, real world and virtual experiences, and inventing the previously impossible, it could be argued that the border between acting in the metaverse and hacking becomes somewhat blurred.

Could I create a game in Roblox, for example, in which players are challenged to hack other player's avatars? Could I create a virtual escape room game, which other avatars literally cannot escape unless they solve my fiendish puzzles? Could I not create an addictive gambling game, in which avatars willingly give up their Metacoin for a chance to win more currency, or some virtual object?

If not, why not? And more importantly, who gets to

decide? If governments and social media companies can't decide who's responsible for taking down hate speech, how are they doing to decide whether my legitimately created game that does 'bad things' should be allowed?

And then it gets ore complex. Who's to say, with my newly learned hacking experience, I can't go and hack another hacker's swindle scheme. Doesn't that make me the good guy? Or is that kind of vigilant activity - good hacking - not allowed either? Again, who gets to decide?

The challenges of artificial intelligence

According to EU human rights organization The Civil Liberties Union for Europe, "simulations show that by 2030 about 70% of companies will have adopted some sort of AI technology. The reason is simple. Whether modeling climate change, selecting job candidates or predicting if someone will commit a crime, AI can replace humans and make more decisions quicker and cheaper."[7]

Any fan of science and dystopian fiction novels and films will be familiar with the idea that one day, the robots will take over. This idea is beautifully exorcised in the original 1998 movie Terminator, when its main character John Connor describes what becomes known in the second film as Skynet: "Defense network computers. New... powerful... hooked into everything, trusted to run it all. They say it got smart, a new order of intelligence." He goes on to say Skynet "decided our (human) fate in a microsecond: extermination."

Terminator 2: Judgement Day puts flesh on those bones. The plot takes place (in August 1997!) as a company technologist is in the final few weeks of reverse engineering a remaining part from the original Terminator (Arnie in the first film). When he completes the task, the program (Skynet) that ran the Terminator becomes 'self-aware' and soon after goes about seeking about the extermination of the human race. A new Terminator is sent back in time by the resistance movement of the future, to prevent this seminal event from taking place.

The key moral point of the film is that government, and public, willingly gave up their systems to artificial intelligence. But the nature of artificial intelligence is that by definition, it can be unpredictable, and also smarter than humans. If it wasn't, why bother at all?

The trope of robots taking over makes for great if chilling entertainment, and certainly doesn't appear to be possible right now. But, the heavy interest and reliance on the potential of artificial intelligence in the metaverse does beg the question of not only what benefits it will bring: of which this book, I hope, illustrates will be many. But also, what challenges need to be planned for.

Artificial intelligence might not seek to destroy humans, but by design it might end up generating outcomes that were not originally envisioned for the metaverse, such as creating bias. It may present only one point of view, fail to interpret human emotions, display serious lack of tact, or have any real interest with the humans it engages with.

Just as right now a robotic artificial intelligence voice, however much its creators claim sounds human, simply doesn't because human voices come with intonations, emphasis, unheard clicks and breaths, that gives confidence and security. Few of us want counseling or sympathy from a robotic voice. Even fewer if we knew it was a robot, going through the motions, and not caring at all. C3PO and R2D2 were sympathetic robots because they were given real human traits and emotions by George Lucas.

Another challenge to AI, at least in the immediate metaverse future, will be that it will be expensive. The rich may get brain implants and expensive augmented glasses with full AI capabilities from the early stages, giving them a head start. The rest of us will have to wait for the hardware and software to become cheap and accessible for all of us to use. They'll get first dibs into exploring the metaverse, using AI to their personal benefit (and perhaps to the exclusion of those who don't share their interests). AI at least in the short term, could increase inequalities and class differentiation.

AI is designed to learn from those who access it. In that case, it will be learning from rich white men right from the start. Mark Zuckerberg, who is pro-diversity in the internet space, admits: "One of the big issues people need to think through is right now there's a pretty meaningful genre skew, at least in virtual reality, where there's a lot more men than women. And that leads to harassment."

Adi Robertson writes in TheVerge: "I understand the reasons for this imbalance, and they're not malicious at all. People quite reasonably test projects on themselves first, and since the modern VR industry skews overwhelmingly male, so do the prototypes. If you can only bring one design to a show, something big will work for more people, even if it works poorly for many of them. That's especially true when the gender gap dictates that most of your visitors will be male. It's a lot of small, rational choices that stack up like bricks in a wall."[8]

By the time the rest have caught up, AI may have learned to react to humans in particular ways that are anathema or even offensive to the rest of us.

A study published in January 2020 revealed that women were more likely to experience sickness than men during a virtual reality experience, because their AI headsets didn't fit properly. When those headsets were adjusted to account for the female face, the difference between men and women and their movement sickness went away. There have been many complaints, from VR headsets to smart watches, that sizing for women has not yet been properly accounted for.

Arwa Michelle Mboya carried out a research project in Nairobi, to explore women's reaction there to using virtual reality to improve their lives. Tellingly, the research was hampered from the beginning, because the VR headsets (Facebook's Oculus GO device, though the author says it could have been any headset) did not fit on many of the women's heads.

"It's not that African women have uniquely big heads. It's that they have uniquely big hair that includes but is not limited to braids, twists, locs, head wraps, and hijabs. Again, not everyone wearing braids or a hijab couldn't put on the headset. But depending on the texture of the hair or how it was tied (or how it was hidden), a good number of participants either couldn't wear the headset or struggled significantly to put it on."[9]

It should be said that AI and the virtual world has lots of potential for helping to reduce inequalities, particularly where it might allow individuals to 'walk in other people's shoes'. These experiences have been used successfully by companies, to help employees understand underlying - as well as overt - racism, sexism, and homophobia.

But at the same time, AI might not be programmed to fairly and sympathetically respond to each and every individual. Whether they can wear an AI headset or not. How far, for example, might AI in a normal game be able to engage with a deaf person, or a wheelchair user, someone with manic depression, or even with someone who has recently experienced a bereavement?

How far will it respect - or even tell - someone's religious, cultural, or societal backgrounds? Some might argue that the benefit of AI is that it doesn't care about a user's cultural background or race. But that will, by default, treat every user as if they were male, white, middle class, able bodied, and straight. We've seen exactly that across physical design, education, gaming, business, and government throughout history. The development of the metaverse will have to work incredibly hard to escape the existing patriarchal, colonial environment in which it is being born.

A final issue with AI might be that it may make human beings insecure. We may be surrounded by beings that are cleverer than us. That will always win an online or virtual reality game. Let's be honest, no-one likes a know-it-all. But that is exactly what AI will be. Fully integrated into the metaverse, we'll be able to access the once satirical all-knowing toaster from the 1990s UK comedy series Red Dwarf (the US version was known as Dwarfing USA) or Deep Thought of the Hitchhikers Guide to the Galaxy.

Like a fully 3D, audible Google, we may no longer be challenged to think for ourselves. It will be outsourced not only by us, but by our kids writing essays or learning their five times table. Will AI write our books? They already correct them. I freely admit to using a program called ProWritingAid to correct my grammar and sentences. AI may produce films, voice overs, avatars, buildings, and learn from everything we do in the metaverse to do it better than we can.

As author Jeanette Winterson puts it in her 12 Bytes, a series of essays about AI and women: "Once artificial intelligence ceases to be a tool, if it does, and becomes a player in the game, something alongside us, then Homo Sapiens is no longer top of the tree."

As already mentioned, the answer perhaps to these AI challenges is legislation. Nowhere in the world regulates AI at time of writing, though other regulations are currently being stretched to cover AI, such as those that govern privacy.

The US government has stated that it wants a Bill of Rights to regulate AI, to ensure that it can't be biased against or for users, and doesn't use algorithms that can't be easily explained.

The Civil Liberties Union for Europe is concerned that facial recognition software, biometric collection and permissions, algorithms, data collection, and other core ideas in the AI aspect of the metaverse will infringe people's right to privacy. The European Union has drafted some legislation, which if passed, will table some use of artificial intelligence as "unacceptable" and would ban them. They include those AI systems considered a clear threat to the safety, livelihoods, and rights of people. It also proposes strict rules on biometrics, such as facial recognition by law enforcement agencies. Companies breaking the rules could face heavy penalties.

The commission's digital chief, Margrethe Vestager, said: "On artificial intelligence, trust is a must, not a nice-to-have... Future proof and innovation friendly, our rules will intervene where strictly needed - when the safety and fundamental rights of EU citizens are at stake." The draft rules face a lengthy approval process and are not yet final.

On September 22, 2021, the UK Government published its ten year strategy on artificial intelligence. The UK is not part of the European Union, and its approach is directly in contrast to the strict one taken by the EU. It notes that the

UK currently regulates many aspects of the development and use of AI through cross-sectoral legislation including competition, data protection, and financial services legislation. It only pledges to look at a proposal in 2022 that sets "out the risks and harms of AI and outline proposals to address them."

Take aways

- There is no clarity on how the metaverse will be governed, or if it will be governed at all.
- The metaverse may offer far wider opportunities for fake news, hate speech, hacking and the dark web, and this needs to be planned for.
- Integration of platforms might make the metaverse more vulnerable to hacking, and also less easy to govern.
- Development of the metaverse may be faster than government's ability to understand and legislate for it.
- The metaverse raises huge questions about freedom of speech, versus protection from harm that will need to be dealt with.

PREVENTING HARMS

When Facebook relaunched as Meta in November 2021, it also restated that it was investing $50 million in research to advise the company how to "build these technologies responsibly." Meta said it would include money to collaborate with industry partners, civil rights groups, governments, non-profits, and academic institutions right from the start.

In its Meta launch video, Mark Zuckerberg meets with former deputy prime minister Nick Clegg 'for a sec' to discuss how "people want to know how we're going to do all this in a responsible way, especially that we play our part in helping to keep people safe and protect their privacy online." Clegg works as VP of global affairs for Meta. He reiterates the point that technology moves quicker than the slower pace of regulation.

Zuckerberg replies that everyone building the metaverse should be focussed on building responsibly from the beginning. He says the company and its partners are focussing on safety, privacy, and inclusion even before the products exist.

Privacy

Are we able to trust that our data and privacy are safe in the metaverse? If the metaverse is any reflection of the internet and social media companies in the past, the answer is an unfortunate but resounding no.

First, Meta (the company behind Facebook) may claim it is good at privacy. But it is not known for putting privacy at its heart, some arguing that profits and spreading its net wider are more important. Certainly, it is difficult to 'leave' the platform we know as Facebook and take all of your private data with you. Do you know how to?

In October 2019, Facebook agreed to pay a £500,000 ($614,500 at the time) fine to the UK Information Commissioner's Office for exposing the data of its users to a "serious risk of harm". The Information Commissioner's Office said the company had allowed a "serious breach" of the law. Google was also caught up in the same data breach scandal.

Live streaming site Twitch says an "error" caused the unprecedented leak that posted vast amounts of sensitive data online. In October 2021, the Amazon-owned platform was breached, including code and documents, as well as the payments made to thousands of top streamers, which was then posted online. Twitch now says the breach was caused by a "server configuration change" that "exposed" some data.

A data 'scraper' managed to take 700 million LinkedIn data records and offered them for sale at $5,000.

On April 3, 2021, Business Insider published a story saying that information from more than 530 million Facebook users had been made publicly available in an unsecured database. Facebook said the data was prior to September 2019, and it had tightened up its software security since then.

Advice is clear: users need to look after their own privacy when entering the metaverse. As it develops, we should look again frequently at the platforms users are already part of, to see what we have given up and what we can grab back in terms of data, permissions, and sharing habits. We may find it's not much, but in a Medium.com blog Lauren Kaufman argues users should look at three aspects.[1]

First, social media companies should be naturally destroying data about us on a regular basis, such as our search patterns and data we store. However, as many have discovered, the internet and social media still remains a venue where even slight whispers of inappropriate language ten years ago, will come back to haunt them. She urges users to take control, so material does not come back.

Secondly, understand what data is being shared among social media and metaverse companies. Whether you've provided information now, in the past, or will in the future, that data might be an asset to the provider which they can sell and share with other platforms, games, advertisers, and more. If you're comfortable with that, fine. But suddenly you may find your own data being used by a platform you've never had any contact with before. If the emphasis of the metaverse is all about shareability and a single united experience, this sharing of data will be vital nutrition for the future internet.

Thirdly, just by using a service, you are giving up some rights to privacy. When we use a card to pay for something we are creating a data trail. Even in the increasingly rare times we pay with cash, we can still be recorded on CCTV, and arguably are giving up some kind of data. Especially if that CCTV has artificially intelligent facial recognition built in. Any interaction in the metaverse may create trail after trail, even if we try to retain as much of our privacy as we can.

The moment we log on to internet browsers, or pull on a VR headset, a new data stream is created that is allocated to a particular device, if not to us as individuals. After even an hour's life in the metaverse, that's a lot of data that will be generated about us, even if we don't share our name, email address, avatar, or anything else.

Indeed, it's harder to see how we will engage with the metaverse at all, if we're unwilling to provide some data, as most of the metaverse will be based on serving our needs, thereby creating more data.

How you feel about your own data - whether ambivalent, or fiercely protective - is your own business. But the commitment of the builders of the metaverse, including Meta (Facebook), is clear: they promise transparency. If we are to give up our data, clear information about how it is used, how it is going to be used, and what might happen if data is breached, should be a cornerstone of our participation.

Ultimately, the question is this: if I use the metaverse, if I share anything about myself, my data, my background, my preferences, if I buy something, visit somewhere in the metaverse such as a gig or a virtual football match, will the data I create be owned by me? Or will it be owned by the platforms I interact with?

Let alone the data you will accidentally capture about other people while going about your own business, even if you've given permission for your own data to be shared. Take the metaverse dream of fully integrated augmented reality glasses. We may love them, and the way they show us lovely data on the inside of the lens. But what privacy do the people we look at have? We could be harvesting, on a metaverse company's behalf, valuable data about *other* people in the same restaurant as us, or on the train, or in our workplace, simply by looking around.

We can look forward to a future where we can't opt out of sharing our data, because lenses are all around us recording it. Or alternatively, we might end up in a world where restaurants, cinemas, beaches, hotels, and even concerts, ban the use of AR glasses completely, to protect the privacy of other customers, to prevent illegal recording, or inappropriate filming.

That would be far away from the sharing experience that everyone in favor of the metaverse has in mind.

Bullying, trolling and hate

Arguably the biggest problem as the internet has developed has been the insipid growth and ease with which users have been able to post content that is hateful, extreme, bullying, and discriminatory.

This has applied in groups, hashtags, YouTube accounts, Instagrams that seem dedicated only to spread hateful messages, usually against a particular minority or 'enemy' groups. And it has been widespread, far wider than the social media companies have been able to control, despite their commitment to do so. They've offered various excuses, ranging from the sheer size of the problem, to fighting back on the grounds of freedom of speech.

But the problem is multiplied in the so called 'dark web', the invisible chunk of the internet protected by passwords, where groups seeking to share illegal activities: from extremist and banned literature, to illegal pornographic materials, extreme homophobic and transphobic exchanges, and even plans for terrorist attacks. Questions have arisen over how far even the social media companies should be responsible at all for this 'dark web', let alone working to restrict access or remove content.

Significant too has been the ability for bullies and trolls to use the internet to target individuals. We've seen this at a celebrity level, from Brittney Spears to the UK's Duchess of Sussex, Meghan Markel. In October 2019, Sulli, former member of K-pop band f(x) committed suicide, widely accepted as a result of continuous negative trolling from social media posters.

Forty-year-old Caroline Flack, the former presenter of the hugely popular reality show Love Island in the UK and a winner of Britain's version of Dancing with the Stars, committed suicide in February 2020. Friends of the presenter accused online trollers, as well as newspapers, for driving her to the action. British Prime Minister Boris Johnson's spokesman called her death a tragedy and said social media companies needed to do more to make sure that robust processes were in place to remove unacceptable content.

These are just some of the higher profile cases. Unfortunately, a young person takes their own life daily as a result of bullying and trolling over social media, or relating to a desire to attain a perfect body, makeup regime, and more expected over social media.

A 2021 study into the significant suicide growth among young women as social media has grown, concluded: "We found that girls who started using social media at two to three hours a day or more at age 13, and then increased [that use] over time, had the highest levels of suicide risk in emerging adulthood."

Sarah Coyne, associate director of the school of family life at Brigham Young University in Provo, Utah and author of the study which was published in Journal of Youth and Adolescence, said: "Research shows that girls and women in general are very relationally attuned and sensitive to interpersonal stressors, and social media is all about relationships."

Over a third of young people between the ages of 12 and 17 say they have been bullied online. Thirty percent have had it happen more than once. About half of LGBTQ+ students experience online harassment, a rate higher than average. Instagram is the social media site where most young people report experiencing cyberbullying, with 42% of those surveyed experiencing harassment on the platform.

The difficulty, of course, is that bullying can be anonymized. It can be intensified, simply by joining in, clicking 'like' or by sharing. By its nature, online bullying can generate a feeling of total isolation, because others avoid posting opposing views for fear of being trolled themselves.

The metaverse threatens to make things worse, not better, if it is not properly governed.

The visual aspect

First, is the visual nature of the virtual aspects of the metaverse. If anonymous trolls are able to use their words and manipulated images to bully right now, how much more available will those mediums be when they can be said in person, through voice disguisers, in a teen or adult's virtual face? How far could an avatar literally 'follow' another's character around the metaverse, stalking their every move, commenting on everything they do? Okay, the victim may be able to 'switch' them off, but we all know that trolls feed exactly off that kind of behavior. One can bet they'll be back, in another guise, to continue the harassment.

Indeed, the UK Daily Mail reported that Meta has already admitted that a 'virtual groping' by a stranger took place during testing of its Horizon virtual reality platform in November 2021. According to a message left by a user on a Horizon hosted talk board for testers of the software, 'Not only was I groped last night, but there were other people there who supported this behavior which made me feel isolated.'

Second, the virtual metaverse will offer all of us another opportunity to 'present' ourselves to the world. There is a risk of pressure upon young men, but particularly upon young women, to look 'great' on the metaverse, as well as in real life. They will need to choose sleek bodies, great makeup, bigger perfectly shaped breasts, and just the right amount of sexy clothing - not too little (slutty avatar), not too much (frigid avatar). In a world where we spend a long tim preparing ourselves to be seen by others, and in some cases just as long for a photo, selfie, or online call with friends, there is a risk that this may be multiplied in an even further visual platform.

In a more complex way, we should not forget the pressure upon all participants in the metaverse to 'normalize' among other participants. It is easy, for example, to imagine that a non-white person in a predominantly white-designed virtual metaverse may choose a lighter color of skin for their avatar, in order to fit in.

In the same way, white and/or powerful people will have

the opportunity to take on skins and actions that do not belong to their natural culture, raising issues of colonialism and cultural appropriation. The old argument about whether a white person should 'black up' will be raised when a metaverse user is able to choose a 'skin' at random, and tailor it to their own particular preference, or for malevolent purposes.

A person who uses a wheelchair may choose to walk in the virtual world. A woman may choose to present as a man, so as to avoid harassment. Those with limbs missing, facial disfigurement, or those living with disabilities may also wish to 'fit in'.

Of course, this would be entirely their choice. Some may be proud of their otherness and want to show it in the metaverse, others may see the virtual world as an escape from some of the limitations they face in the real world.

The nature of one's desire to 'fit in' only emphasizes, and perhaps encourages, the idea that there is an 'ideal' body, gender, skin color, and ability that we should all be seeking to attain.

Bullying

And that's before the bullying. In a world where woman receive regular trolling because of their body shape or even face on social media, how much more vulnerable will individuals be for what they choose to wear or how they appear in virtual worlds? Even what shops they choose to enter, or activities in which they'd like to participate? We could be adding a whole new layer of expectation to those who are already basing much of their lives in meeting assumptions placed on them by society.

On Fortnite, kids often complain about being singled

out as a 'newbie' on the platform, because every new starter is given a basic combat fatigue skin: a 'default'. There's nothing worse than being a 'default'. They can only upgrade their skin by winning battles or spending real money. Kids report being bullied online because of their low grade costumes and find themselves targeted by those eager to win easy points by shooting down newbies in the game. Now, Fortnite is more of a social platform than a gaming one, the opportunity to shame and make fun of those in lower level skins are rife. The only option, for someone who wants to 'shine' or even become invisible to haters, is to buy expensive skins. Too much like real life?

Offensive behavior

The visual aspect of the metaverse offers extremists of all colors and creeds a perfect opportunity to display their wares. Once again, there will be far more opportunities than the words and flat images and videos of today can convey.

There will be no reason, for example, why avatars can't make a Hitler salute? Or a rude gesture? Or why a user cannot develop a virtual skin that others find offensive, such as that of a slave trader, or neo-Nazi or a suicide bomber.

There could be offensive protests outside of virtual mosques, churches, synagogues, temples, political meetings, abortion advice centers, and more. How physics will work in the metaverse is yet to be decided, but will an avatar be able to physically prevent another avatar from moving around and into these virtual buildings?

In the virtual world we may be able to get away with far more than we are allowed by our own democracies, because with four billion people online, it will simply be too large to police. Indeed, it would be impossible without some hard-coded rules in the metaverse, where it is simply not possible to display a Nazi salute. But if that's the case, who gets to make the decision about what's allowed and what's not? And what if a certain gesture is fine in one country, but not in another?

And while the dark web is likely to remain in its current form, invitations and knowledge on how to access it are likely to become easier to come by, simply by people's larger access to the online world.

Mark Zuckerberg envisages a world where we spend up to 80% of our day inside the metaverse, either in a virtual or augmented platform, or otherwise interacting. If in my own internet daily experience, I'm only a few mis-keys or spam emails to content I do't want to see, how much more available will those opportunities be over a full day, totally immersed?

Mitigation

What are the social media companies and the drivers of the metaverse promising on these issues? In his launch video of Meta, Mark Zuckerberg doesn't mention bullying, trolling, or hate speech at all, nor does he mention it in his interview with TheVerge.

In a statement on the Meta website, it says: "We have developed AI systems that can identify many types of bullying and harassment across our platforms. However, bullying and harassment is a unique issue area because determining harm often requires context, including reports from those who may experience this behavior. It can sometimes be difficult for our systems to distinguish between a bullying comment and a light-hearted joke without knowing the people involved or the nuance of the situation."

It says that much of the policing will be done by AI, though policies are drawn up in partnership with interested parties. It also says it relies on users to report abuse, and to protect themselves through the use of unfriending, unfollowing, and blocking accounts.

While the commitments feel real, some might argue Meta is giving itself plenty of wriggle room by arguing it relies on user reporting and AI to seek and delete offensive and bullying content.

According to Forbes magazine: "Facebook employs about 15,000 content moderators directly or indirectly. If they have three million posts to moderate each day, that's 200 per person: 25 each and every hour in an eight-hour shift. That's under 150 seconds to decide if a post meets or violates community standards."

Compare that with the 10,000 new employees Meta is about to recruit across Europe solely to code the virtual platform of the future, to accompany another 10,000 people working on augmented and virtual reality projects in its Reality Labs division.

Epic Games, which runs Fortnite, has freely accessible Community Rules banning bulling and harassment, as well as intolerance and discrimination. It urges users to use its in-player reporting tool to call out those who don't 'play nice', and instructs how players can block another player - even if they're not breaching community rules.

In Minecraft, one form of bullying, called grieving, is when a player purposefully destroys what another has built, or steals their stuff. This can be frustrating for players, whose hard work can be destroyed quickly or just want to play building by themselves.

Minecraft is clear about what it will allow and what it won't, including "repeated and unwelcome aggressive acts against an unwilling and non-consenting player, who has priorly asked the aggressor to leave them alone." They include attacking another player if they have not asked to be in a player vs player state, killing a player's animals, following a player around, or behaving in a threatening manner, even if no actual combat is initiated, and finally, Minecraft: "take a very dim view of anyone attempting to organize coalitions or gangs for the purpose of disrupting other players' enjoyment of the game, or harassing individuals."

In the metaverse, these and other rules may have to be reshaped, and new ways of detecting problems and enforcing solutions and bans will need to be developed. They will have to ensure tackling the problem of bullying and antisocial behavior stays ahead of the development of the platforms, rather than as it has been in the past, trailing behind.

Other harms

Addiction

According to US statistics agency Statista, at least 16% of American 13 to 17 years olds report 'almost constantly' being on social media, with another 27% being on social media every hour. That survey, the latest comprehensive and trusted survey, was in 2018, well before the idea of the metaverse became well spread.

If the principle of the metaverse, as stated by expert Matthew Ball, is that it will be ever-present and continuous, we can fairly suspect the 'always on' culture among young people, and adults, will continue to rise.

Facebook's own research, quoted by the Wall Street Journal, reveals that more than 12% of users "report engaging in compulsive use of social media that impacts their sleep, work, parenting, or relationships."[2]

Whether one calls this addiction or not might be debatable, but it is certainly true that being online, in a headset, prevents all users from doing something else. And social media use has been shown to increase depression, lessen attention outside of social media, and to increase health problems.

In a world where we're already checking our mobile messages from the moment we wake up until we go to bed, and where we swap out walking, exercise, and even shopping to do so online, there is a real danger of public health implications in the future of the internet.

Depression

A study of a number of papers about social media and adolescents' mental health, concluded in 2020 that "extensive research on the quantity and quality of SM [social media] use has shown an association between SM use and depression in adolescents... At the same time, some aspects of SM use may have a beneficial effect on adolescent well-being, such as the ability to have diversity of friendships and easily accessed supports. Furthermore, the use of SM content to detect symptoms has potential in depression and suicide prevention... Since SM will remain an important facet of adolescents' lives, a better understanding of the mechanisms of its relationship with depression could be beneficial to increase exposure to mental health interventions and promote well-being."[3]

As these are new technologies, there are no long-term studies of their physical and psychological effects. Even less, any speculative material about the effects of the metaverse in the future.

But as the study acknowledges, the link between social media and living online and depression, anxiety, and even suicide, can be linked in a non-causal relationship. There is not yet enough research to signify a causal link. It adds that dopamine messes with our ability to time how much we've been involved in social media.

What might be noted, however, is that social media and partners in the metaverse may need to look closely at their platforms, and support further research into this area, and to adopt their offerings appropriately.

Physical health

At the very least, it has been proven that a static lifestyle, including one of poor health and fitness, and poor diet, can lead to depression and anxiety, as well as serious health issues like heart disease and cancer. Add to this our increased distance from real relationships with other people, the breakdown of the social life we all need. Many have reported that, despite the hype, social media makes people feel more lonely. The metaverse will not just change the way we interact with the internet and our devices; it will change how we interact with each other.

It is not hard to estimate that the metaverse may encourage this kind of lifestyle for some, even though it may also provide better opportunities for others to exercise, connect, and build a healthy diet.

Phil Reed is a professor of psychology at Swansea University, in the UK. He told the London Evening Standard: "If you think of the [massively multiplayer online] games, where people immerse themselves in landscapes... they get huge amounts of reinforcement from being in that landscape, that they're not necessarily getting outside, and that encourages them to spend more and more time in that fantasy landscape because, if your life outside is not very nice, so you're probably going to go where the reinforcement is."

Once again, legislators may need to work together with the companies behind the metaverse, to ensure that a burden of ill health does not fall on governments as a result of living lives almost entirely online.

Take aways

- There are questions about our privacy and security of data in the metaverse.
- The nature of AR generates serious concerns about privacy for those who do not wish to share their data.
- Bullying and trolling are likely to be magnified in the metaverse, and will be different.
- There is a danger that programs and equipment will initially be designed for white middle class, 'normal' men.
- Long periods in the metaverse are likely to create physical and mental health problems among users, especially for those excluded in wider society.

FURTHER CHALLENGES

The metaverse offers unprecedented opportunities for the future. In one way or another, it will touch every one of us: whether we engage with the platforms through work and education, through health and well-being, through creating and earning, or simply through our leisure time.

It is easy to be cynical, because some of the companies that have put their weight behind the future of the internet - in terms of money and branding - have let us down before. Nevertheless, we use their products every single day, and most of us are excited with what they are offering us into the future.

The number of times over the writing of this book that I have read accusations of this or that company 'conveniently' making noise about the metaverse so as to divert us from this or that criticism doesn't ring true.

The invention of the metaverse has been long term, and its vision has been decades in the making. As commentators have said throughout this rise in interest, the metaverse has been developing for a long time, we just didn't call it the metaverse.

It will continue to develop in a way where we won't, at any point, be able to say: here it is. And it will become so much part of our lives, that we no longer call it the metaverse at all, but instead look to the future in a completely new way as yet not even conceived.

With that in mind, however, we as users, as well as looking to governments and policy makers, must ensure that metaverse leaders keep their promises about privacy, safety and not exploiting users. We will continue to offer our privacy and data in a fair exchange for the tools we want to use, but as we do so, it is important that the very platforms we will increasingly rely on allow open debate and criticism of them so at to keep them in check.

It is not enough for metaverse platforms to claim 'we don't know yet' about issues of child protection, data capture, hacking, and policing rights and responsibilities in the metaverse. Especially while at the same time they are promoting all the great things these platforms are theoretically going to do for us.

Every step forward in technical development will need to bring with it reassurance. That never happened with the internet, leaving governments and companies chasing their tails, with serious implications such as extremism and suicide. That cannot be allowed to happen again.

This author suggests the following will be the immediate short-term challenges for the metaverse companies, and for us as consumers, to consider as the metaverse develops.

True creative freedom

One of the attractive elements of the metaverse has been the leaders' commitment to an open platform, where each of us users can be creative and inventive within the platforms, to generate our own ideas and contribute to the future. In the past, some social media companies have been predatory, buying up tools and programs, creating monopolies and stifling freedom to create. A change of perspective will be needed, so that those who create continue to own their intellectual property, and that design and create platforms don't contain hidden clauses that transfers that intellectual property to the platforms without their owner's consent.

The challenge of interoperability

To be new and useful, the metaverse will have to be significantly different from the internet and Apps we all currently use. We can just about hang on to the dozens of passwords we use to access different profiles and accounts. If the metaverse repeats that mistake, it is unlikely to take off. But that challenge of interoperability will not be easy, particularly when we are just as concerned about privacy and security as we are about remembering a few different account logins.

The metaverse must be open to all comers

Already, the faces popping up in favor of the metaverse have been the usual stereotype of white men from the higher income world, and male gaming geeks. In this progressive society, we may need to be convinced that the internet of the future is not only designed for those who don't fit into those shoes, but also by them.

In particular, the question of how those who live in the lower- and middle-income world will be engaged as partners in the development of the new internet, not just 'grateful' recipients of tools we believe they need.

The environment

The metaverse must enable action on, not distract us from, other vital issues.

In a sense, the move towards more screen time, more distant interaction, more electronics, and more ways to invest and make money does not chime well with some other priorities in society right now, including the environment, climate change, our desire to live 'slower', and shop locally with lower impact than before.

While we might be tricked into thinking we're supporting local and artisan suppliers, we may yet be increasing plastic, shipping, and other CO_2 hungry processes.

Being human

Instant messaging, email and social media posts have taken us away from face-to-face contact. But many would argue that being physical and intimate with each other is what makes us human. The metaverse will need to facilitate better human contact, not reduce it, if it is to become a positive in many people's lives.

Privacy and data

Evidence shows that users do want to know what they are exchanging their private data for, and how their data is being mined and used. They want to know how to remove themselves from platforms, and to gain their data back. And some want to know what platforms are offering them in exchange for their data, from free Apps to actual monetary value. Promises to protect our privacy and data aren't enough. We will need to see clear descriptions of how this takes place, and be able to make informed choices about what we will lose if we don't give our permissions.

Walking into progress?

There is a temptation for all of us, already deeply embroiled into social media and internet tools, to do nothing. Every commentator has said the metaverse will develop slowly, there will not be one day when we 'opt in'. Over the next few years, we'll obediently tick the update box on the Apps and programs we use, and will happily see the metaverse develop without even noticing it. Soon we will find ourselves as ensconced in the future of the internet without knowing how we got there. It is worth therefore continually, or at least once a year, asking ourselves: how much do we want and need what is being offered to us? What are we willing to sacrifice, and where do we draw our red lines?

Do people actually want the metaverse?

According to a September 2021 survey of internet users in the US, 39% of responding adults thought that social media was bad for society. Overall, only 22% of respondents thought social media had a good impact on society.[1]

Sometimes happenstance occurs. We are offered something we didn't know we wanted, and it works. Facebook is perhaps the biggest winner in that game. But its dominance has meant others have turned away from the platform, or have questioned its dominance.

Other grand plans on the internet have fallen flat within years, or even months. The biggest early success of the internet was boo.com. It was launched in the autumn of 1999 selling branded fashion. The company spent $135 million of venture capital in just 18 months, and went bust in May 2000. There's hype and there's reality.

Facebook and the other metaverse companies have money to invest, and investors who believe in their dream. But their version of the internet will live or die according to whether people actually use their tools, want what they're offered, and find it preferable to the current status quo.

The English proverb goes: 'necessity is the mother of invention'. The jury is currently out about whether we need to go into a virtual world to have meetings, or even to play games, or to attend gigs and sport, when those things are all perfectly possible, desirable, and satisfy the human condition in the real world already.

Is the metaverse offering something we never knew we needed, or will it reach the hyped-up heights that have been promised of it?

And so, we land back in the world of gaming, where desire to try new things and adopt new platforms is the lifeblood of the industry. In his arguably equally prescient and qualified article for PCGamer.com, Wes Fenlon writes in *The metaverse is bullshit*:

"Tech companies are now spending billions of dollars

straining against that basic fact: for most of what we do online, sitting at a monitor and typing is going to be the most practical interface for a very long time."[2]

The next ten years are sure to tell if what is on offer is what we want.

Thank you for reading ***Your Life In The Metaverse***. I hope you enjoyed the experience and the content, and are looking forward to finding out more about the subject.

It would mean a lot if you felt able to review this book on your usual platforms, and also to share about it on your social media.

If you would like more information about the author, please visit me at www.gideon-burrows.com

You can also visit me at my own social media.

Thanks again,
Gideon Burrows

ACKNOWLEDGMENTS

Thanks to Matthew Ball and John Radoff who have written extensively on the metaverse, in detail and with passion. I can thoroughly recommend their websites at matthewball.vc and jradoff.medium.com.

Thank you to Simon Whittacker for supporting all of my work, and to Sarah Mole and Iain McFarlane for being part of my editing and proofing team. Thanks to my Alpha readers for giving the book its first look over.

PORTICO

"Pacy, thrilling, suspenseful and complex to keep your attention... this is a must-read for anyone who likes intelligently-written thrillers - political, techno, or otherwise." ★★★★★

"The best of this genre I have read for a long time." ★★★★★

"A thought-provoking thriller. I'm already casting the film version in my mind." ★★★★★

It's 2030. A world of driverless electric cars, touchless screens and social media that knows what you want before you do.

When jaded journalist Curtis Soren meets the new powerful boss of the government's mysterious Ministry for Society, he uncovers a top-secret organisation that puts him and his colleagues in danger - and threatens the privacy and freedom of every citizen.

In a struggle with his own haunted past and a present he doesn't understand, Soren is forced to take on Portico, the biggest social media organisation of all.

It becomes a desperate battle to expose the truth in an online world of fake news, censorship and social users addicted to their screens.

Lose yourself in this thrilling page turner which will challenge how you think about the future, and what you might need to sacrifice to get there.

https://books2read.com/u/mq0w7Q

FUTURE SHOP

Rosa Bodran is in a rush as usual.

The ferocious weather is doing everything it can to prevent her getting on with her day.

A strange man offers her a virtual reality shopping experience, guaranteeing it will be quicker, easier and cheaper than her usual family shop.

It'll mean she can pick up her kids on time, despite the freezing hail and wind.

But all is not as it seems.

Futuristic shopping might not be the solution to Rosa's problems.

It could put everything she cares for at risk.

Dive into this mystery futurist thriller, and face some of the deepest question about how you want your own future to look like.

From the award winning author of Portico and The Illustrator's Daughter, comes a short book that shows this challenging writer at the cutting edge of what he does.

https://books2read.com/u/4jo5qZ

REFERENCES

Introduction

1. https://www.youtube.com/watch?v=OKnpPCQyUec
2. https://en.wikipedia.org/wiki/Metaverse
3. https://medium.com/building-the-metaverse/9-megatrends-shaping-the-metaverse-93b91c159375
4. https://www.theverge.com/22588022/mark-zuckerberg-facebook-ceo-metaverse-interview
5. https://www.washingtonpost.com/opinions/2021/07/28/will-metaverse-connect-us-or-just-remind-us-how-far-apart-we-remain/
6. https://www.bbc.co.uk/news/technology-58749529
7. https://www.matthewball.vc/all/forwardtothemetaverseprimer
8. https://www.mindmeister.com/2025115594/metaverse?fullscreen=1

Exploring the metaverse

1. https://www.axios.com/metaverse-creator-neal-stephenson-facebook-name-change-a4259282-5016-4c67-a7ae-b0eb381a7773.html
2. https://medium.com/building-the-metaverse/9-megatrends-shaping-the-metaverse-93b91c159375

The metaverse now

1. https://www.mindmeister.com/2025115594/metaverse?fullscreen=1

What hardware will you need?

1. https://labs.thinkbroadband.com/local/broadband-map#5/-89.848/158.840/
2. HighSpeedInternet.com
3. https://www.theverge.com/22588022/mark-zuckerberg-facebook-ceo-metaverse-interview

Artificial intelligence

1. https://medium.com/building-the-metaverse/9-megatrends-shaping-the-metaverse-93b91c159375

Money

1. https://www.coindesk.com/markets/2021/07/17/how-axie-infinity-creates-work-in-the-metaverse/

Work

1. https://hbr.org/2020/08/research-knowledge-workers-are-more-productive-from-home

Education

1. https://en.unesco.org/icted/content/lifeline-learning-leveraging-technology-support-education-refugees
2. https://www.youtube.com/watch?v=7zAohS3X50Q
3. https://www.fenews.co.uk/skills/british-tech-companies-making-the-tech-education-and-training-metaverse-a-reality/
4. https://www.kaist.ac.kr/newsen/html/news/?mode=V&mng_no=13771

Health and medicine

1. https://www.thelancet.com/journals/lanonc/article/PIIS1470-2045(21)00148-0/fulltext
2. https://www.forbes.com/sites/saibala/2021/10/30/facebooks-evolution-into-meta-has-incredible-potential-to-revolutionize-healthcare/?sh=534aad4d5c5f

Social media, leisure, and gaming

1. https://www.theverge.com/22588022/mark-zuckerberg-facebook-ceo-metaverse-interview
2. https://www.dailymail.co.uk/femail/article-10309237/Couple-met-online-holds-virtual-wedding-metaverse-simultaneously-marrying-

real-life.html
3. https://www.nme.com/features/gaming-features/porter-robinson-virtual-festival-2929407

Governance and democracy

1. https://www.washingtonpost.com/video-games/2020/04/17/fortnite-metaverse-new-internet/
2. https://www.raphkoster.com/2021/10/14/object-behaviors-how-virtual-worlds-work-part-4/
3. https://www.nytimes.com/2021/10/29/technology/meta-facebook-zuckerberg.html
4. https://medium.com/berkman-klein-center/the-metaverse-a-brave-new-virtual-world-2f040cbae7d4
5. https://research.umd.edu/news/news_story.php?id=13541
6. https://www.nortonrosefulbright.com/en/knowledge/publications/5cd471a1/the-metaverse-the-evolution-of-a-universal-digital-platformv
7. https://www.liberties.eu/en/stories/ai-regulation/43740
8. https://www.theverge.com/2016/1/11/10749932/vr-hardware-needs-to-fit-women-too
9. https://debugger.medium.com/the-oculus-go-a-hard-ware-problem-for-black-women-225d9b48d098

Preventing harms

1. https://lolokaufman.medium.com/the-metaverse-privacy-you-998e002f687b
2. https://www.wsj.com/articles/facebook-bad-for-you-360-million-users-say-yes-company-documents-facebook-files-11636124681
3. https://www.ncbi.nlm.nih.gov/pmc/articles/PMC7392374/

Further challenges

1. {$NOTE_LABEL}. https://www.statista.com/statistics/1268213/us-opinion-on-social-media-good-or-bad/
2. https://www.pcgamer.com/the-metaverse-is-bullshit/

www.ingramcontent.com/pod-product-compliance
Ingram Content Group UK Ltd.
Pitfield, Milton Keynes, MK11 3LW, UK
UKHW021650190726
13853UKWH00001B/170

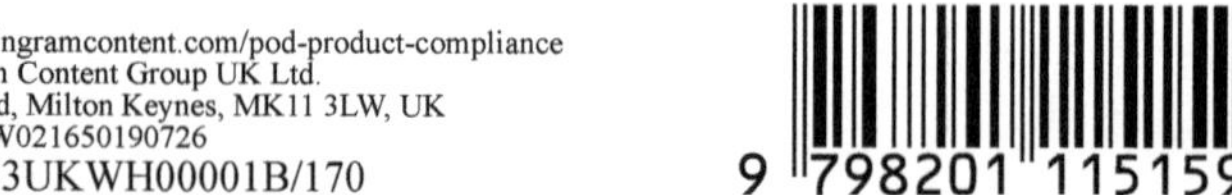